IMAGES
of Modern America

JACKSONVILLE

On the Front Cover: Clockwise from top left, singer Kris Allen, an American Idol star, attends a fundraiser at Excell Park for the Boys and Girls Club (see page 93, courtesy of the Jacksonville Historical District); Harlem Globetrotter "Firefly" Tay Fisher visits Pathfinder Lighthouse Charter School while student Camryn Williams helps him spin the ball (see page 29, courtesy of the Jacksonville Historical District); Splash Zone Water Park is one of many great attractions in the city (see page 78, courtesy of the Jacksonville Parks and Recreation Department); Tonyville Merchantile is located in the Tonyville community (see page 11, courtesy of Leonard Carmen); the Red Devils storm the field (see page 35, courtesy of Jacksonville High School).

On the Back Cover: From left to right, the front window of the H&H Barbershop is captured by the camera (see page 71, courtesy of Patrick Thomas); Col. Patrick Rhatigan lays a wreath on Memorial Day (see page 55, courtesy of Little Rock Air Force Base); this is an exterior shot of the family-owned Adams Foreign Car Repair (see page 64, courtesy of the Jacksonville Historical District).

IMAGES of Modern America

JACKSONVILLE

Barbara Mashburn and Brianna Mashburn

ARCADIA PUBLISHING

ISBN 978-1-4671-1480-6

Published by Arcadia Publishing
Charleston, South Carolina

Printed in the United States of America

Library of Congress Control Number: 2015937930

For all general information, please contact Arcadia Publishing:
Telephone 843-853-2070
Fax 843-853-0044
E-mail sales@arcadiapublishing.com
For customer service and orders:
Toll-Free 1-888-313-2665

Visit us on the Internet at www.arcadiapublishing.com

To the Jacksonville Historical District members: their hard work and love of our local history has made this preservation of our town possible.

Contents

Acknowledgments

Special thanks to local residents for their love of our city's history; the Jacksonville Military Museum; Jacksonville Historical District members; the *Leader* newspaper; local artist RB McGrath; local historian Carolyn Yancey Kent; Otis Stewart Jr.; Jill Ross (human resources); Susan Davitt (city clerk); Mayor Gary Fletcher; Jay Whiskers (engineering); my daughter Brianna, who has spent many hours researching the history of each photograph to make this book a wonderful tribute to our city a success; my son Brian; my daughter Nicole; my grandchildren; and many others who have helped with the information and photographs.

A very special thanks goes to Arcadia Publishing for giving us the opportunity to express our city in a pictorial book and everyone who has offered their help with photographs and historical information with this collection. We are a proud city of rich history.

INTRODUCTION

The Jacksonville-Gray Township area originated in the winter of 1820–1821 at two important crossroads: the Southwest Trail that went north and south, and the Memphis-Military Road that went east and west. Stagecoaches came soon after the roads were passable, and the community at that point boasted a tavern, stagecoach stop, and school.

In 1870, a railroad line cut through the small community on land owned by Nicholas Jackson, where a depot was built, and Jacksonville then became a city. The community evolved from the settlement surrounding the railroad depot, eventually incorporating in 1941. The population soon climbed to 200 and maintained that number until a large ordnance plant was built during World War II. The footprint of this plant included much of present-day Jacksonville and employed close to 20,000 people.

Recognized throughout the state as Arkansas's fastest-growing city, the migration northward from the congestion of the larger cities to this bustling center of suburban activity has recorded an astounding contemporary history in growth and development. The popularity of this small town has made it the ideal place to live and work. With the advent of the nuclear age, Jacksonville took its place as a member of the giant Strategic Air Command family of the free world with its neighbor the Little Rock Air Force Base, one of the finest defense facilities in the nation.

The opening of the Little Rock Air Force Base complex in such close proximity to Jacksonville resulted in tremendous growth and a building boom. The city's leadership, with keen vision and sound backing, advanced with the population. Retail sales climbed to a record peak. The new Jacksonville highway, linking the city to the metropolitan area via the multimillion-dollar interstate highway system through central Arkansas, makes it possible to commute to the opposite edge of Pulaski County in a span of about 20 minutes. Construction of new homes and development of new subdivisions throughout Jacksonville are evidence of the tremendous growth of the town.

Development of the industrial park and relocation of a dozen major industries there added still more strength to the solid backbone of the rising economy, with its openings of available sites continuing to attract businesses seeking greener pastures. Municipal services were expanded to meet the demands of the new era with the creation of a city-planning commission and broadening police and fire protection as well as other related activities.

From its beginning prior to the Civil War, when settlers from Eastern states arrived to take advantage of the fertile upland soil and numerous springs and were joined by residents of what are now Little Rock and North Little Rock who fled the ravaging floodwaters of the Arkansas River, Jacksonville has been born and reborn into a prosperous, thriving city.

As the years have gone by, Jacksonville has faced many periods of adversity and prosperity, but citizens have never lost faith in their community and have rallied to help neighbors continue to cultivate the town. This book focuses on the town from the 1960s to the present and includes the Jacksonville Historical District, located on Second and First Streets, a tourist attraction featuring the original train depot near its original location. Many thanks is given to Mayor Gary Fletcher for his help in locating the old train depot and reacquiring it for the city for residents to enjoy. We look forward to the new stores that are in the older buildings on First Street with the opening of the historical district. So come visit and enjoy coffee and Wi-Fi in beautiful historic Jacksonville.

The people who have grown with the town of Jacksonville cherish it dearly among their own accomplishments and passions. Without the dreams and visions of residents and elected officials, this would not be the great town of Jacksonville, Arkansas, that is loved dearly by lifelong residents.

The photographs in this book show the growth that has been experienced by the town for over 50 years, such as the Museum of Military History that is home to every branch of the military and their history; the Reed's Bridge Battlefield Heritage Park, where a re-enactment takes place every year of the battle that was fought there in 1863; Southern Oaks Country Club, with its manicured 18-hole course; Splash Zone Water Park, Jacksonville's largest aquatic center, with two pools, one of which is perfect for the smallest of visitors; Dupree Park, which is the largest of nine parks located throughout the city; and the Arkansas Game and Fish Commission Gun Range. These are just a few of the many various wonders within the city limits.

One

Restaurants and Retail

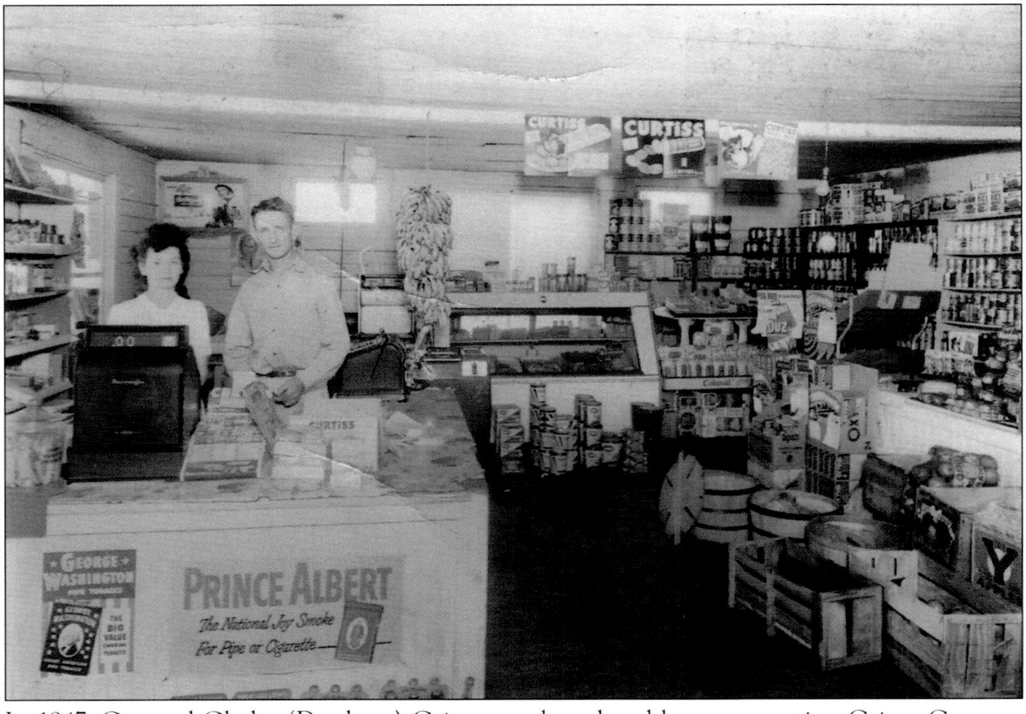

In 1947, Gus and Gladys (Dunham) Griggs purchased and began operating Griggs Grocery, located at Oak and East Main Streets. Prior to acquiring the store, Gus worked at the Arkansas Ordnance Plant and farmed in the early 1940s. He also was a volunteer fireman for the City of Jacksonville. They lived at 408 Hickory Street with their children: Kenneth, Francis, Mary, and Donald. Gus passed away on January 25, 1992. (Courtesy of the Griggs family.)

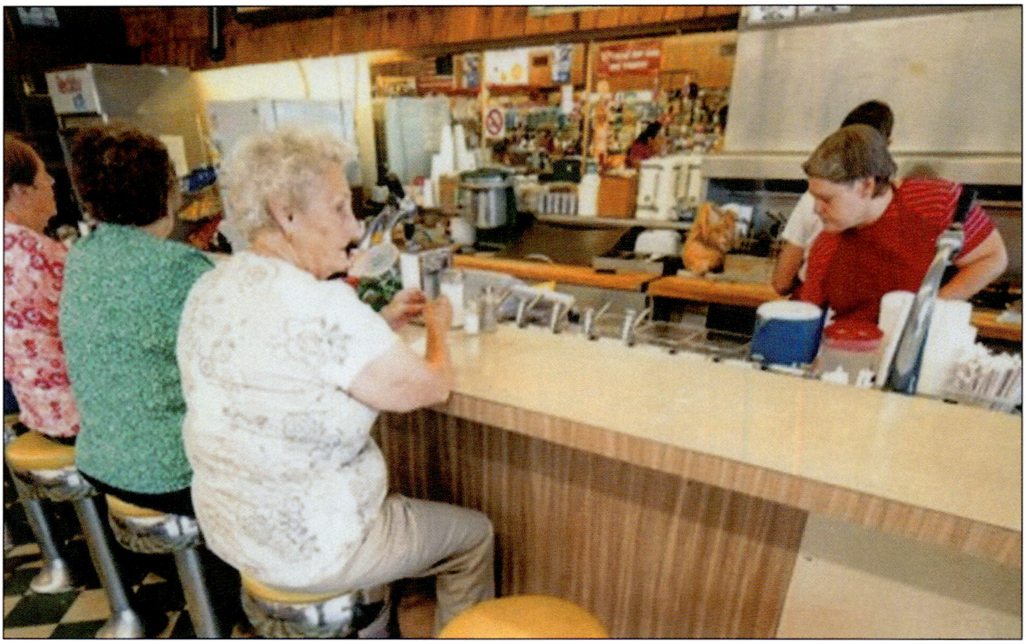

Chambers Drug Store was the only pharmacy in town that mixed its own prescriptions from the doctor. Bill Chambers and his wife, Pat, owned the soda shop and drugstore when it opened in 1956. In 1975, the business was purchased by Ron Lukas and Gayle Fowlkes. By 1985, Lukas was the sole owner of the popular shop. Above, from left to right are, Beth Furlow, Jo Beatty, Geraldine Reschel, and Vera Wilkerson sitting on the original bar stools at the soda fountain. Below, patrons sit at the counter with town historian Otis Stewart Jr. (second from the left). (Courtesy of Otis Stewart Jr. and Ethel Lyons.)

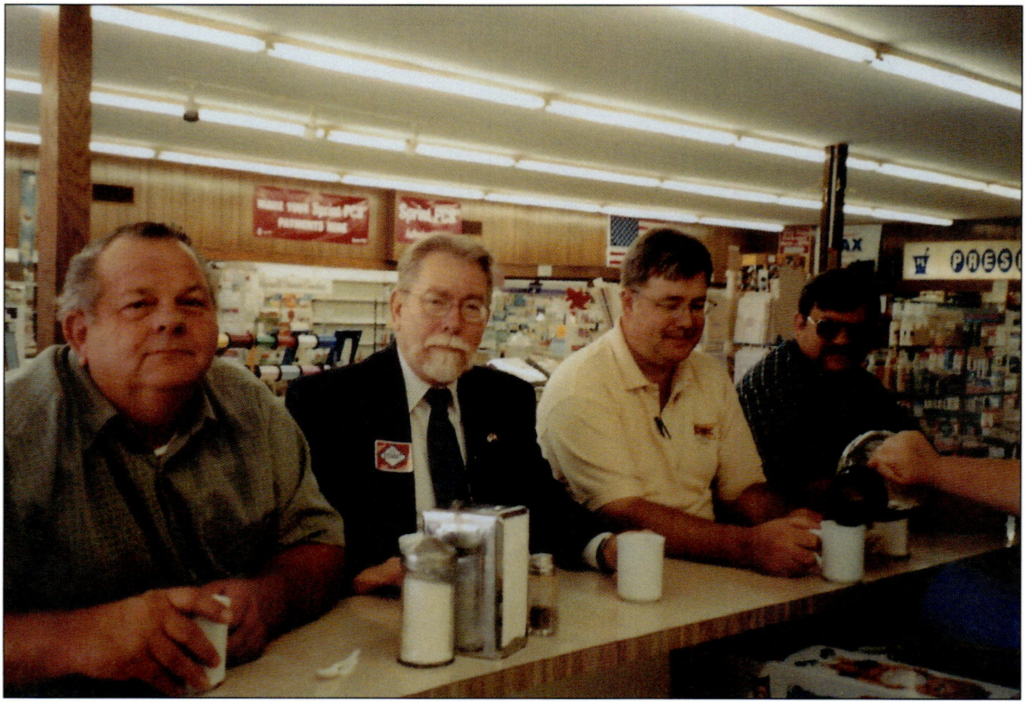

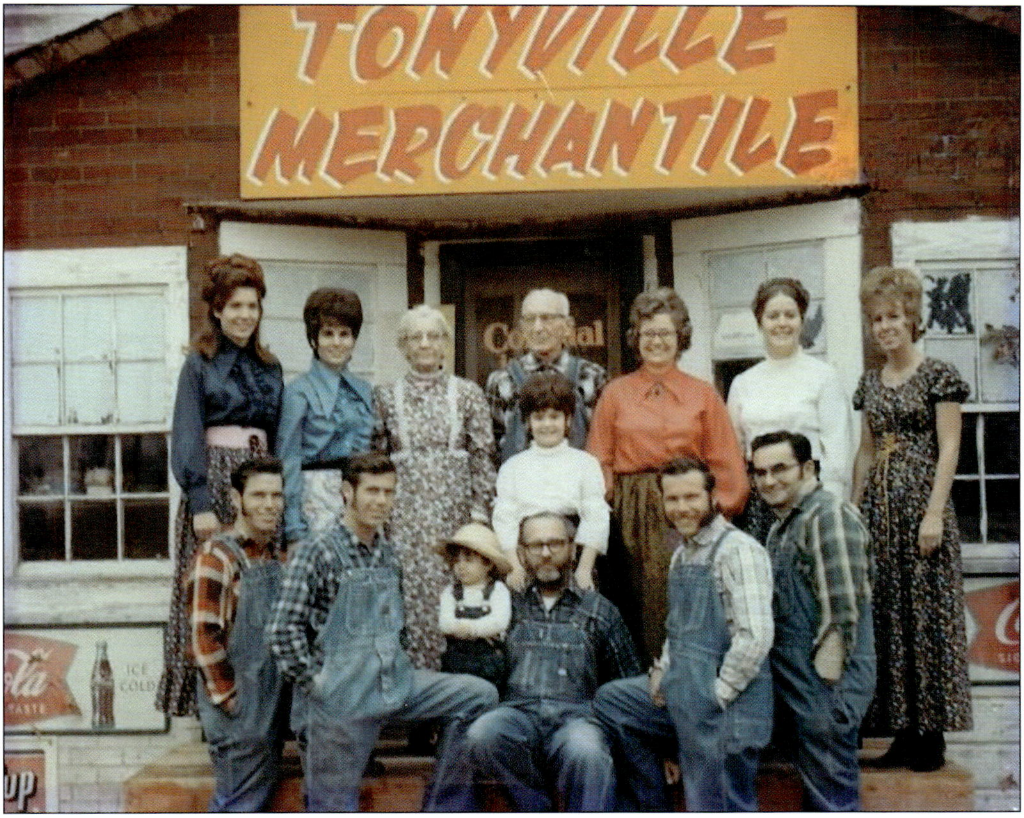

The Mashburns were the first owners of Tonyville Merchantile, which opened in 1964, but Chuck and Dot Drummond took over the business with their family in 1969. Leonard, the little boy in the straw hat, thought it was fun to pump gas up into the glass container at the top of the pumps, which held 10 gallons. After years of business, the building has seen its better days, as evidenced below, and is now a reminder of what once were happy times for merchants and customers. (Courtesy of Leonard Carmin.)

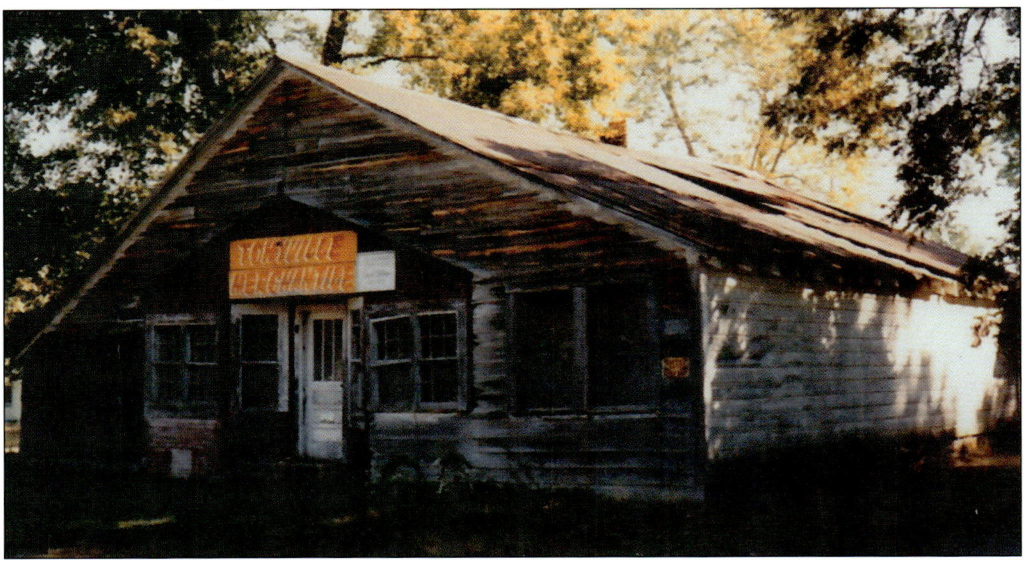

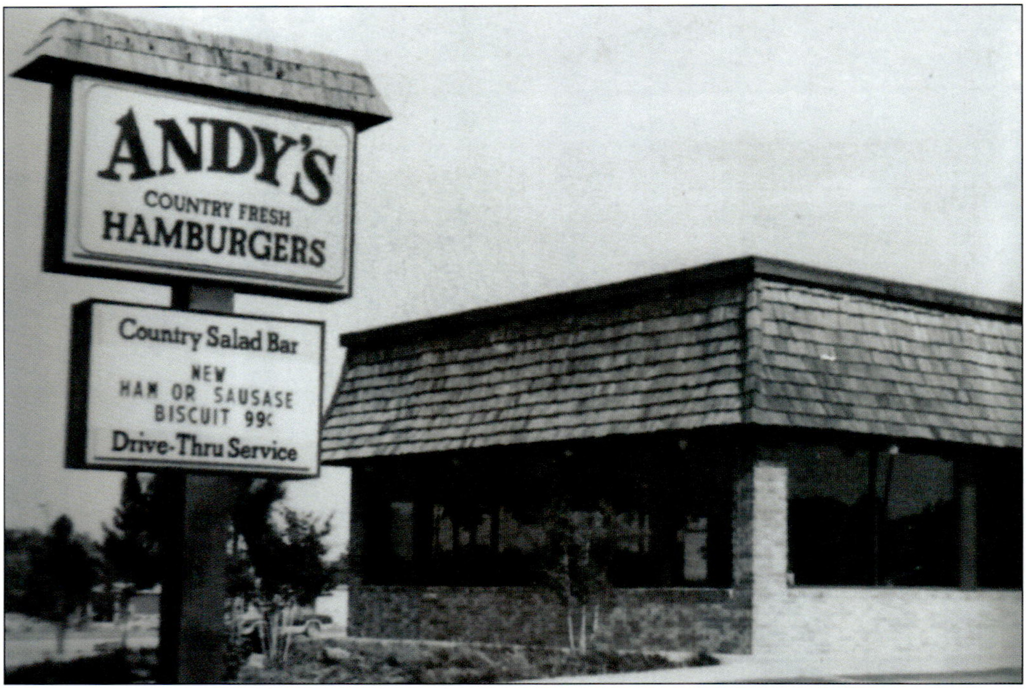

Andy's Burgers, "Home of the Hometown Burger," opened in 1978 and closed in 1989. It was located on T.P. White Drive, close enough to Little Rock Air Force Base and the high school. Andy's was a favorite place to eat for years; the building is now the home of the Original Fried Pie Shop, which serves both sweet and meat pastries. (Courtesy of the Jacksonville Historical District.)

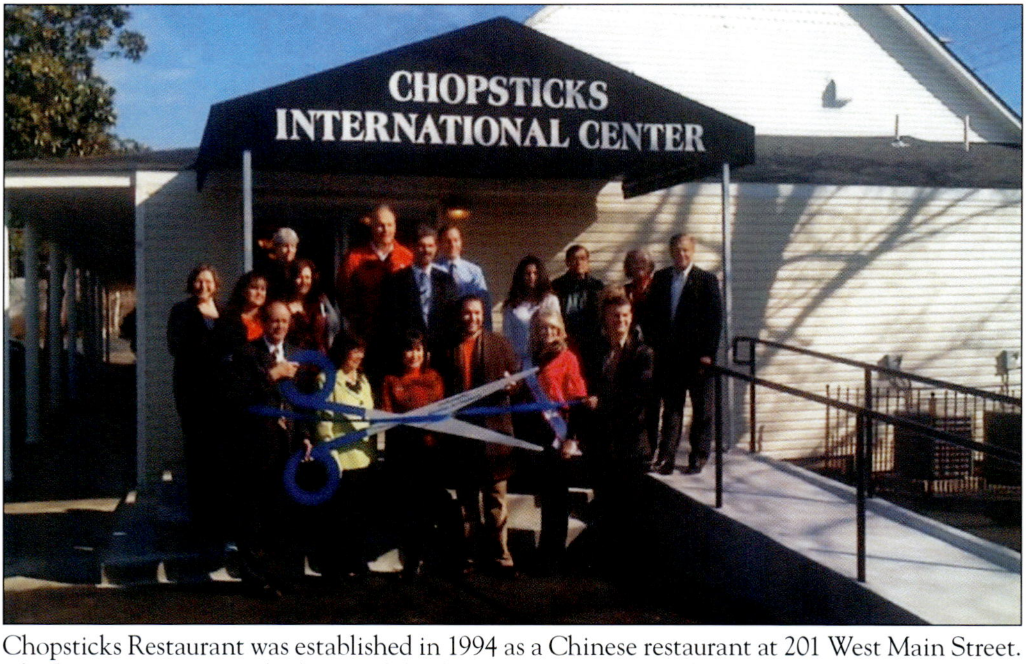

Chopsticks Restaurant was established in 1994 as a Chinese restaurant at 201 West Main Street. The location was once the home of the first mayor of Jacksonville, John H. Bailey, who served in 1941 and 1942. In 1956, it was home to the local newspaper *Daily News*, owned by James and Catherine Canfield. (Courtesy of the Jacksonville Historical District.)

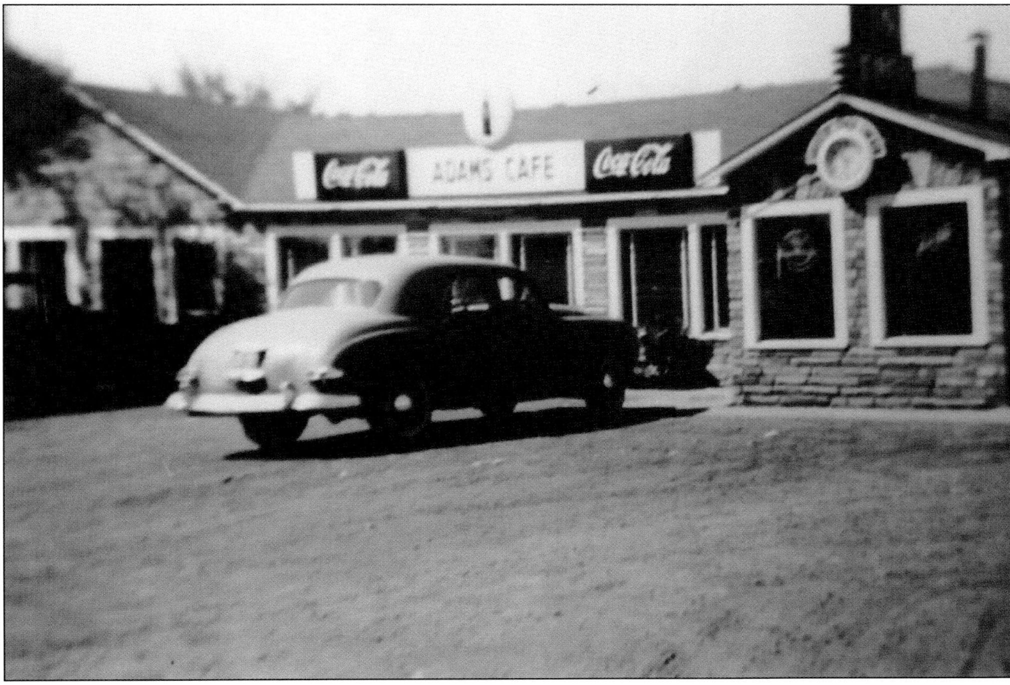

Adams Café was owned by M.J. "Bud" Adams and his wife, Louise (Stanphill) Adams. In the 1930s, this café was located on Graham Road across from the railroad tracks, but it moved to two different locations on Highway 161 in the early 1960s. Louise was immensely poplar for her delicious, crispy fried chicken; on some days, they would pack 250 fried chicken dinners for the ordnance plant workers, priced at 75¢ a plate. (Courtesy of Patty Peters.)

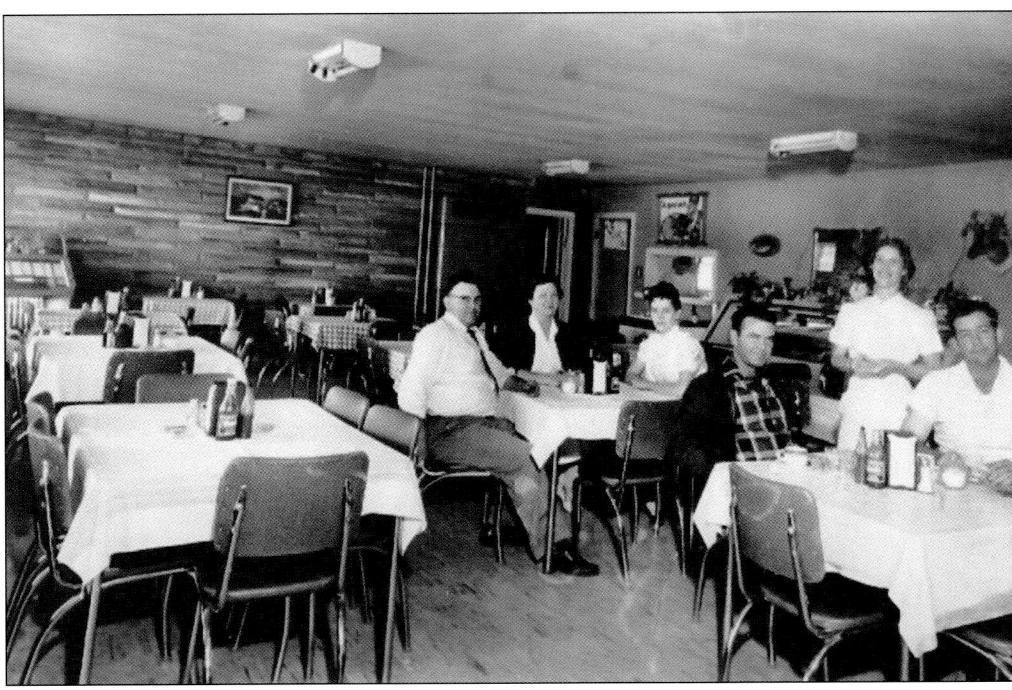

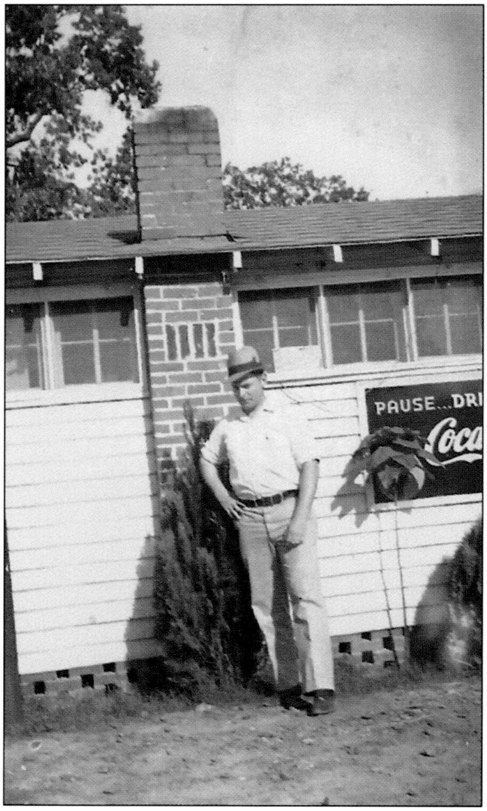

At left, Bud Adams is pictured standing beside his café on Highway 161. Adams retired in 1960. His wife, Louise, pictured below, was popular for her fried chicken, and many nights she would stay late at night to cut up fresh chicken for the next day. (Courtesy of Patty Peters.)

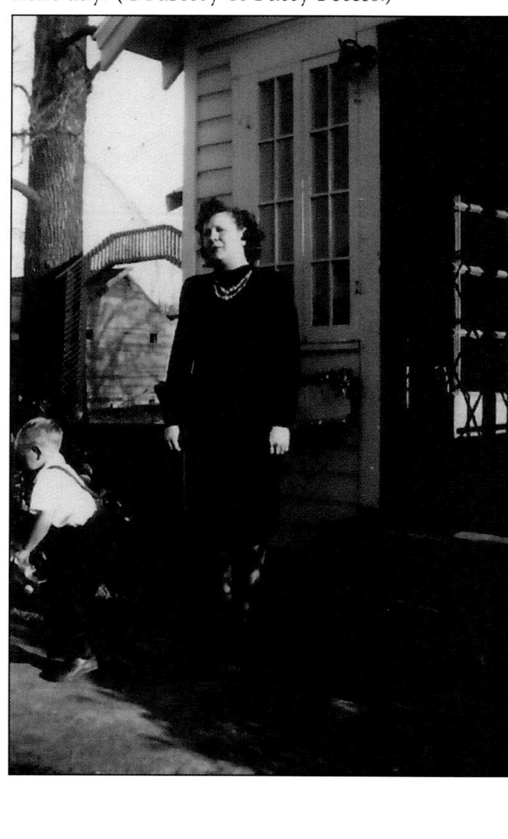

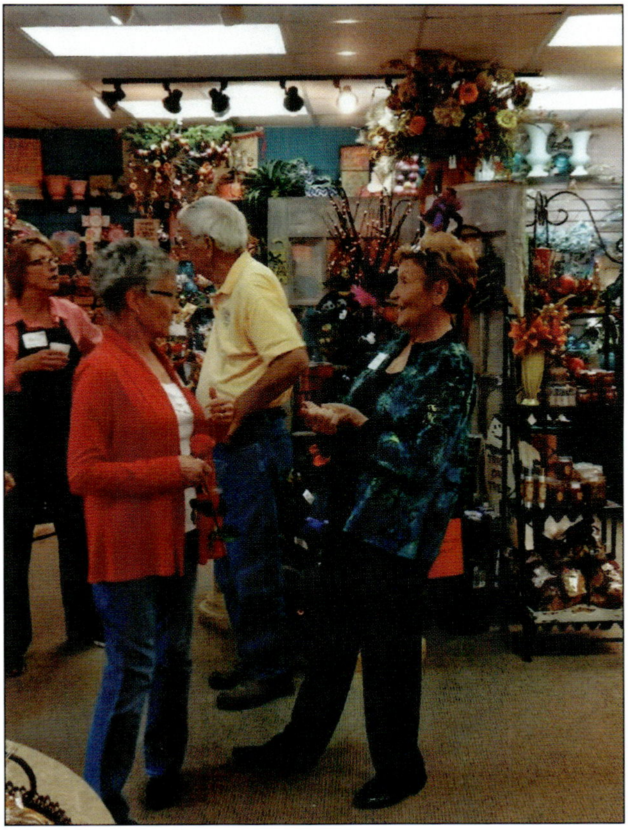

In 1964, Virginia and Bill Frizzell were on their way to a Razorback football game when they noticed the Double R Florist and Gift Shoppe was for sale. They opened for business that year, where the old police department detectives' offices are now, and in 1972 they moved to their present location at 918 West Man Street. In 2014, the business celebrated its 50th anniversary. (Courtesy of Double R Florist.)

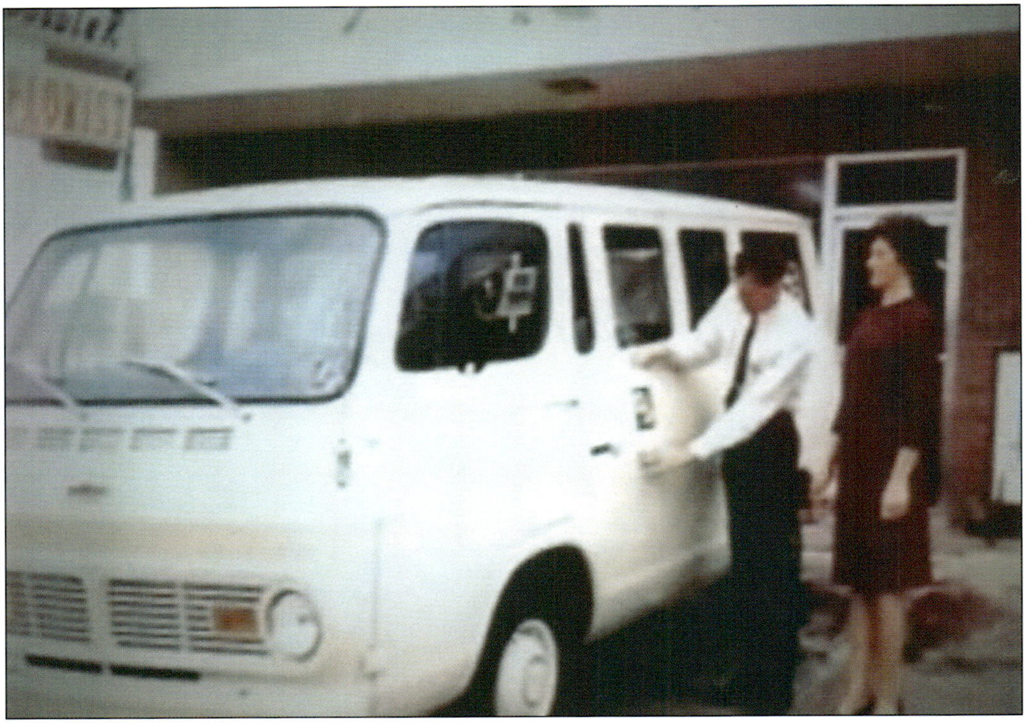

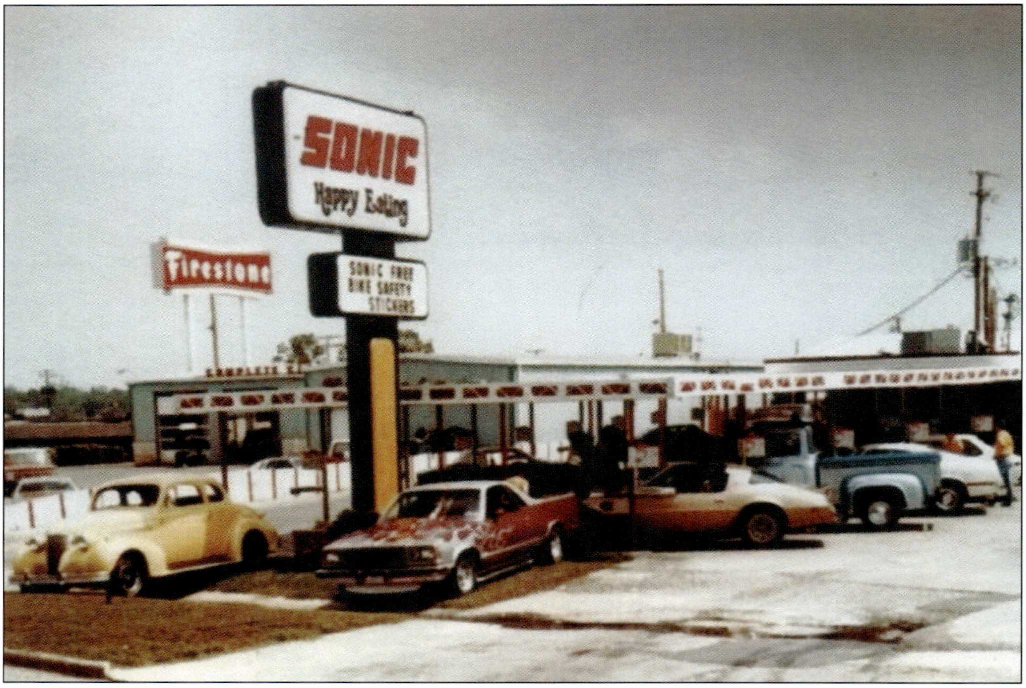

Sonic Drive-in, located at 1010 West Main Street, opened in March 1972. As one of the few fast-food places around that stayed open late, it was the favorite hangout of teenagers in town. (Courtesy of Wanda Sanders.)

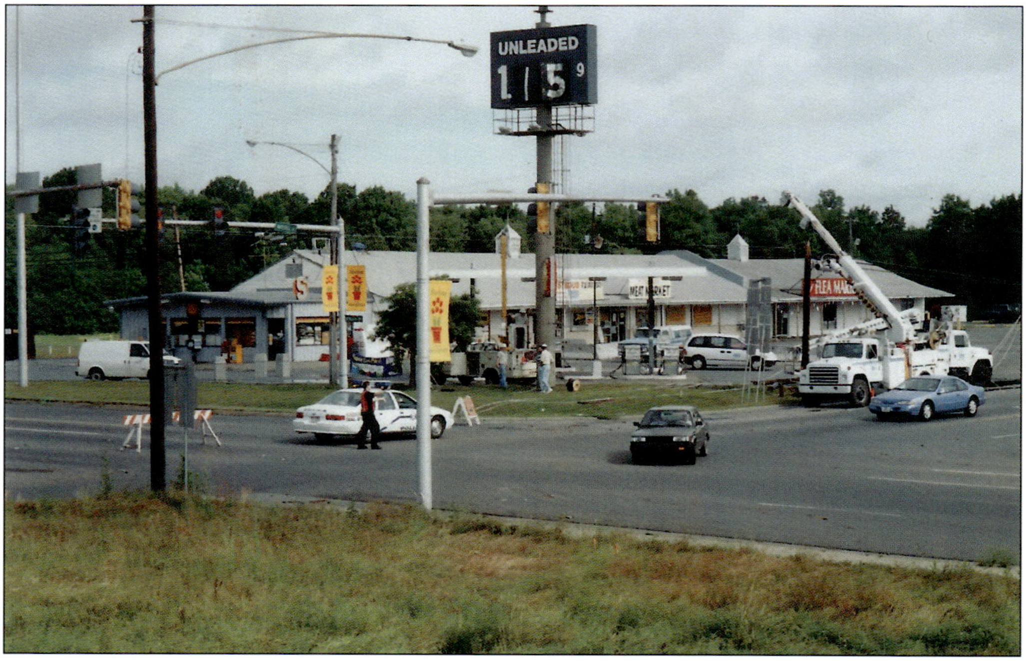

Pictured here in the 1980s is the shopping center on Marshall Road and Main Street, with the Shell station, Stroud's TV, and Floyd's Meat Market in the background. This plaza was torn down to make way for the Chili's restaurant that sits here today. (Courtesy of the Jacksonville Historical District.)

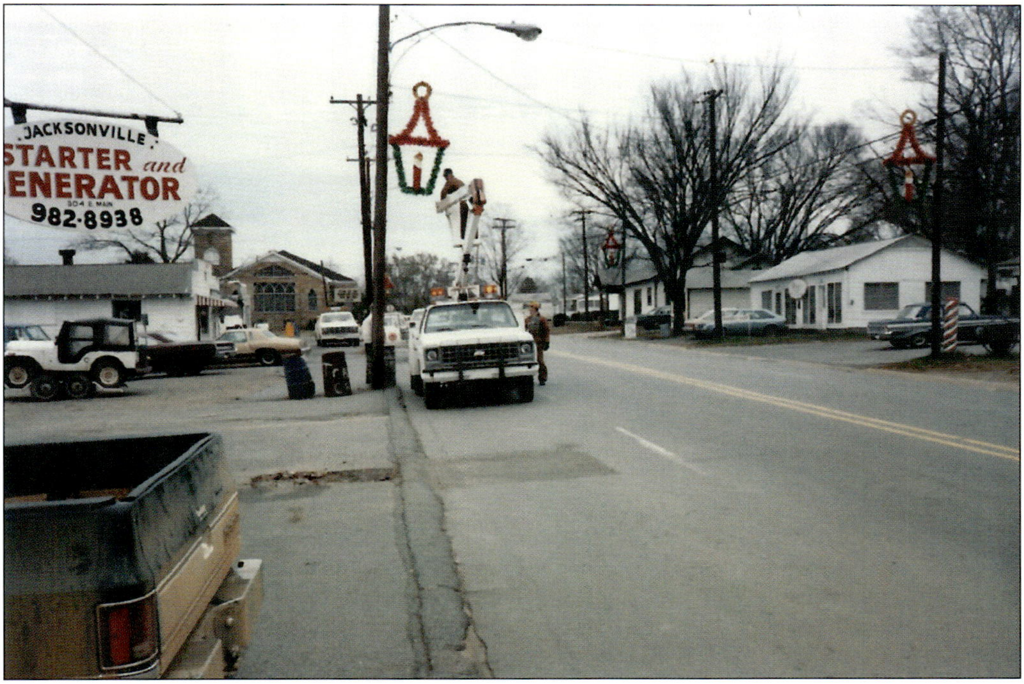

Jacksonville Starter and Generator shop, pictured here in the 1980s, is owned by Johnny James. The family business was established in the 1960s on East Main Street, and it thrives today, with his Johnny's son running things after his retirement. (Courtesy of the Jacksonville Street Department.)

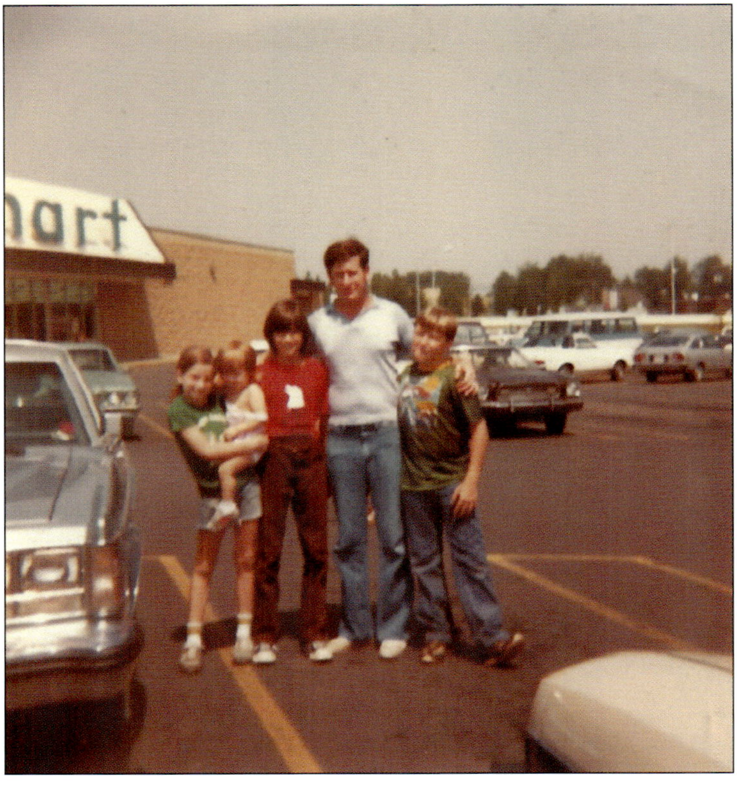

From left to right, Hollie (holding Michelle), Doyne DeVinney, Bill, and Heath Bolton are pictured standing in the parking lot of a Kmart. This store opened in the early 1970s closed in the 1980s. (Authors' collection.)

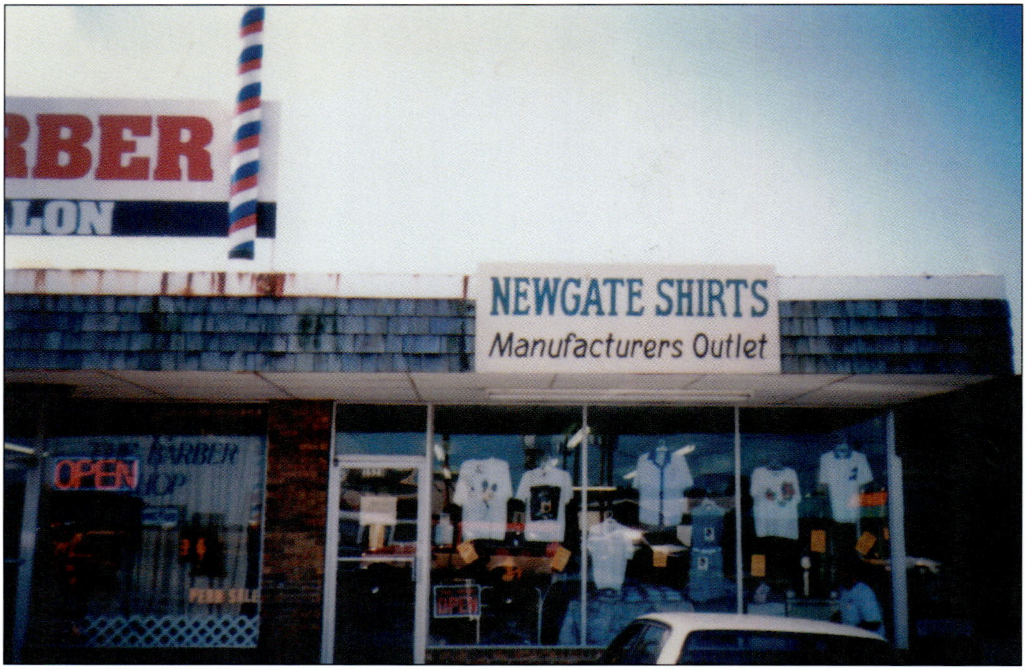

Newgate Shirts, built in 1959, is located inside a shopping center on Main Street. Over the years, several businesses also in the shopping center included a barbershop, a military recruiting office, and The Diner. This is one of the first small shopping centers one sees when coming into town from the freeway. (Courtesy of Charles Wilson.)

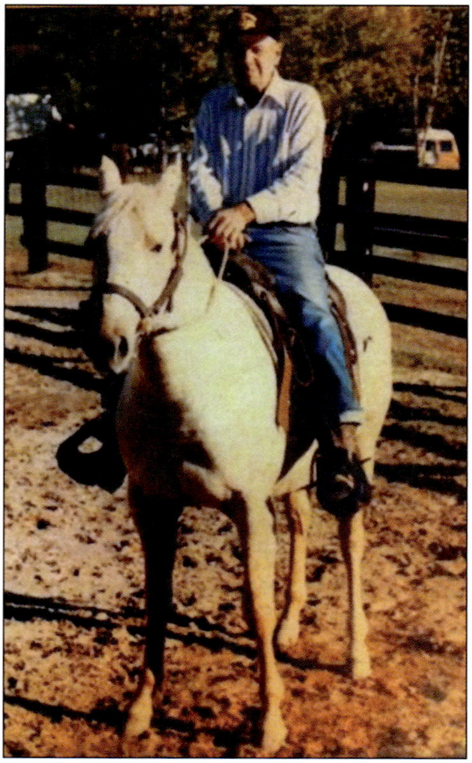
Tate Taylor is pictured on his horse Zero. He was well known in Jacksonville by teenagers because he maintained a huge swimming hole that they would use. Taylor also loved animals; he even had a raccoon named Bandit that slept in a doghouse. (Courtesy of Tommy D. Wolf.)

Two

CHURCHES AND SCHOOLS

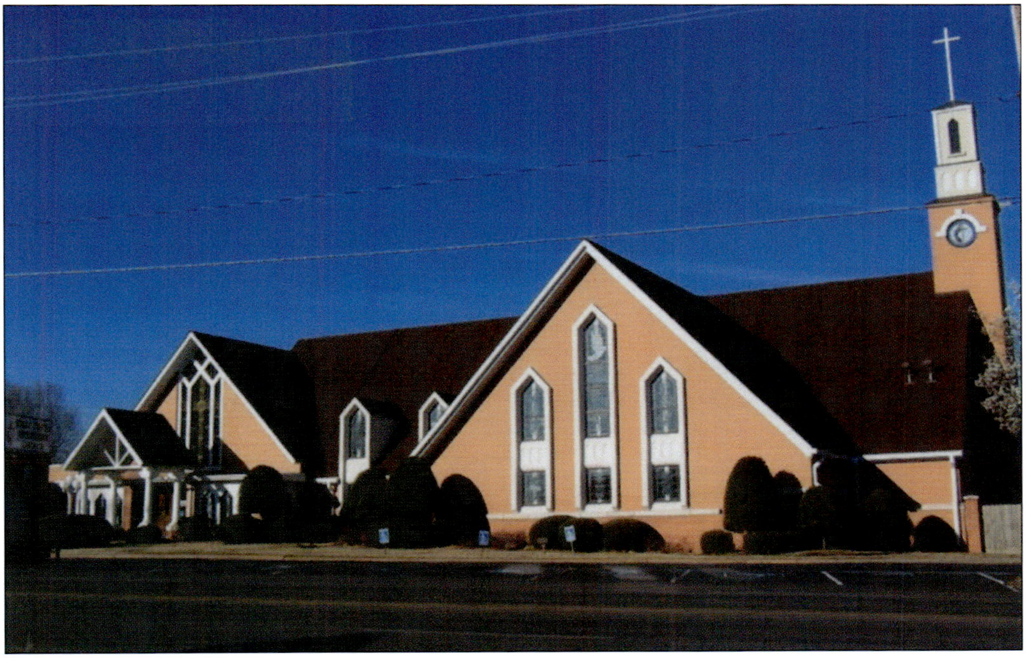

In 1880, First United Methodist Church was a two-story log structure that was also used as a community building and as the first public school in the area. The Masonic Lodge would hold its meetings on the second floor. By 1883, the congregation built a new church, located at 220 West Main Street, using logs from the old church. Elias Wilson hauled the logs and new lumber in an oxen-drawn wagon. The new building was erected with free labor on land donated by Joseph B. Gray and his family, and it had two front doors: one for men and one for women. Inside were three rows of pews: one for men, one for women, and the middle for children. The original structure has been remodeled several times over the years. In the 40 years from 1938 to 1979, the church was on a circuit with other Methodist churches in the area with student pastors from Conway traveling to preach on weekends. Since 1950, the ministers have been seminary-trained men. (Courtesy of First United Methodist Church.)

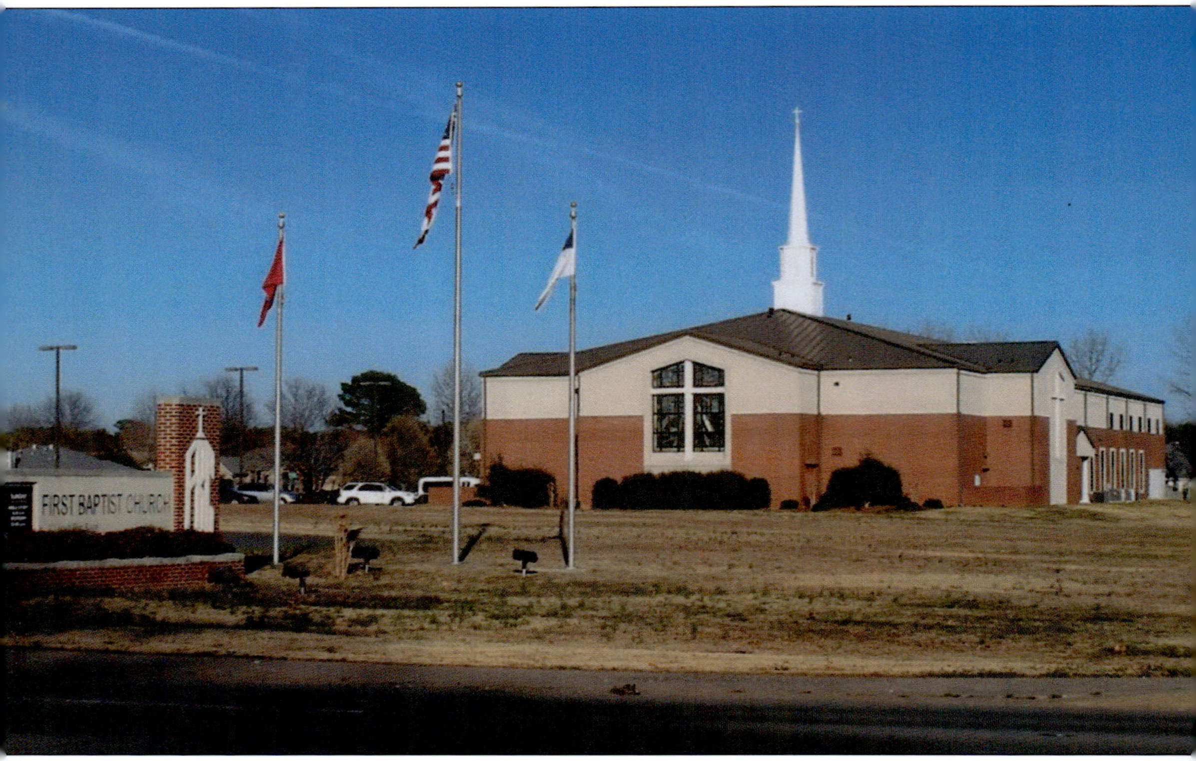

First Baptist Church, currently located 401 North First Street, was established on May 4, 1872, with James M. King and J.P. Eagle as the ordained ministers. Services were first held in the building that is now occupied by Evangelistic Ministries Church, located at Main and Elm Streets. The church included Elder R.P. Bain, acting chairman, and Elder W.E. Corder, acting clerk. The last 55 years have seen many changes to this church. On August 16, 1901, the congregation passed a resolution that the church would move four miles northwest to New Bethal School House. It was at this location until 1921, when a new church was built by the members using donated material sawed by the Shell Thompson mill. (Courtesy of the Jacksonville Historical District.)

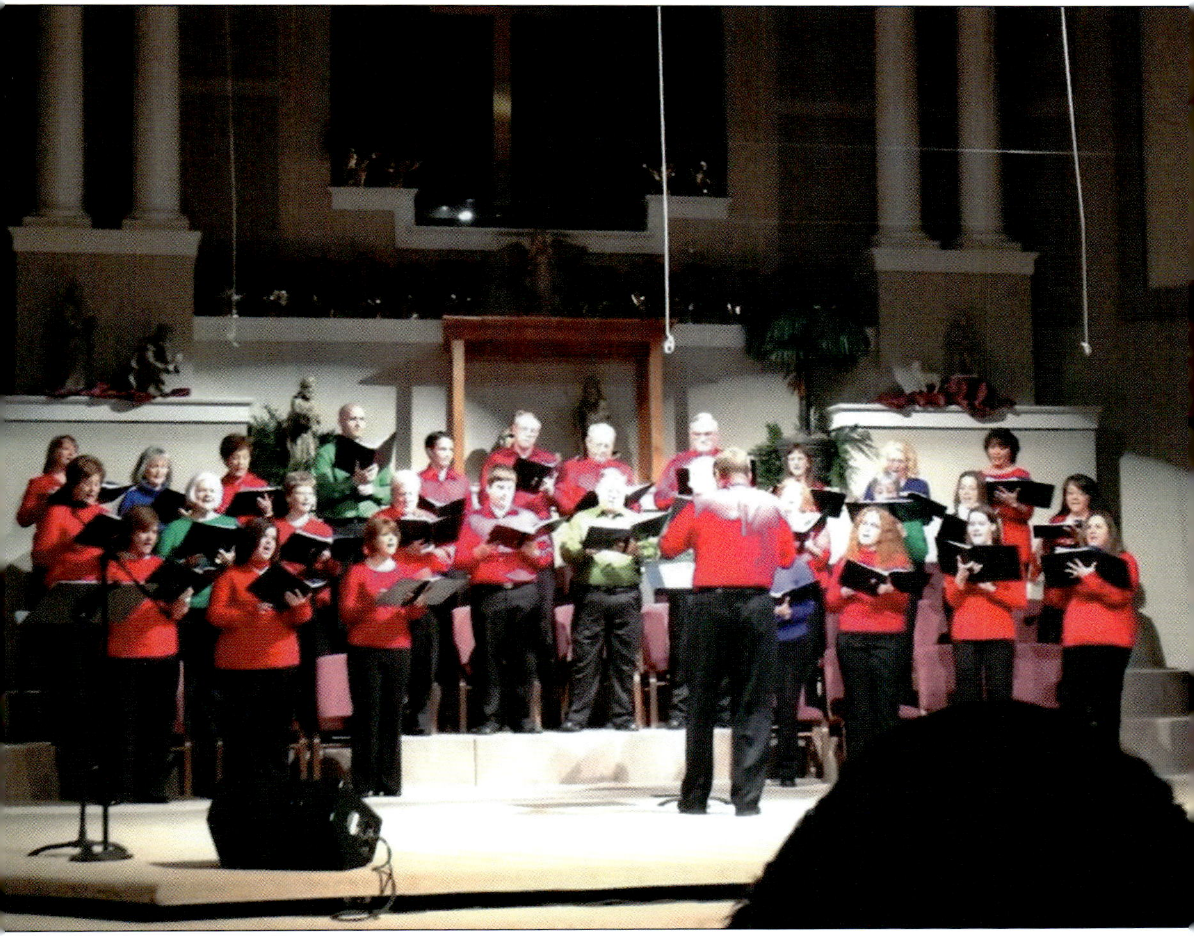

The 30-person choir at First Baptist Church is singing for the holidays in front of the congregation. This is an annual performance by members of the church in celebration of the Christmas season. (Courtesy of the Jacksonville Historical District.)

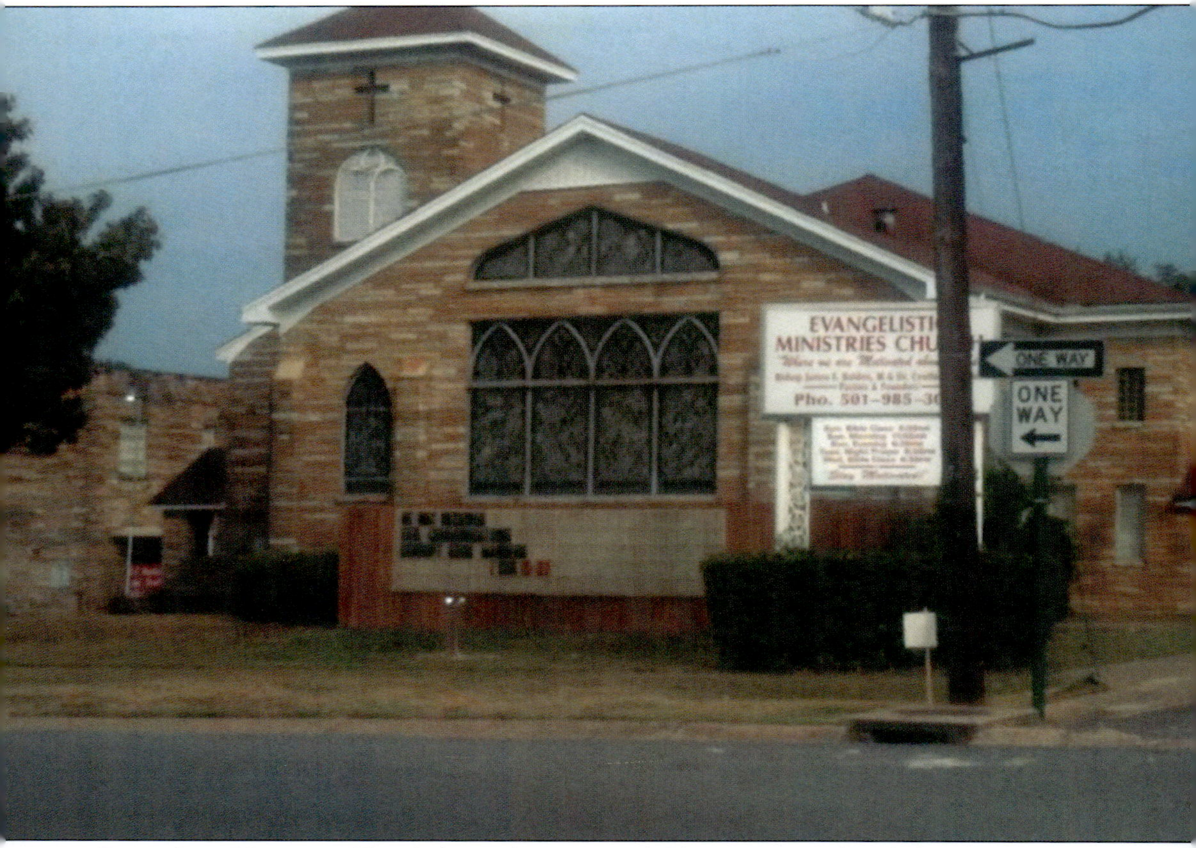

Evangelistic Ministries Church, located at 101 North Elm Street, was founded in 1996 by Bishop James Bolden III and Lady Cynthia E. Bolden. Bolden started DIVA (Disciplined, Intellectual, Victorious, Anointed, Sisters) for Christ in 2002 as part of this ministry. A Baptist church was previously at this location, but the congregation moved into another building. (Courtesy of the Jacksonville Historical District.)

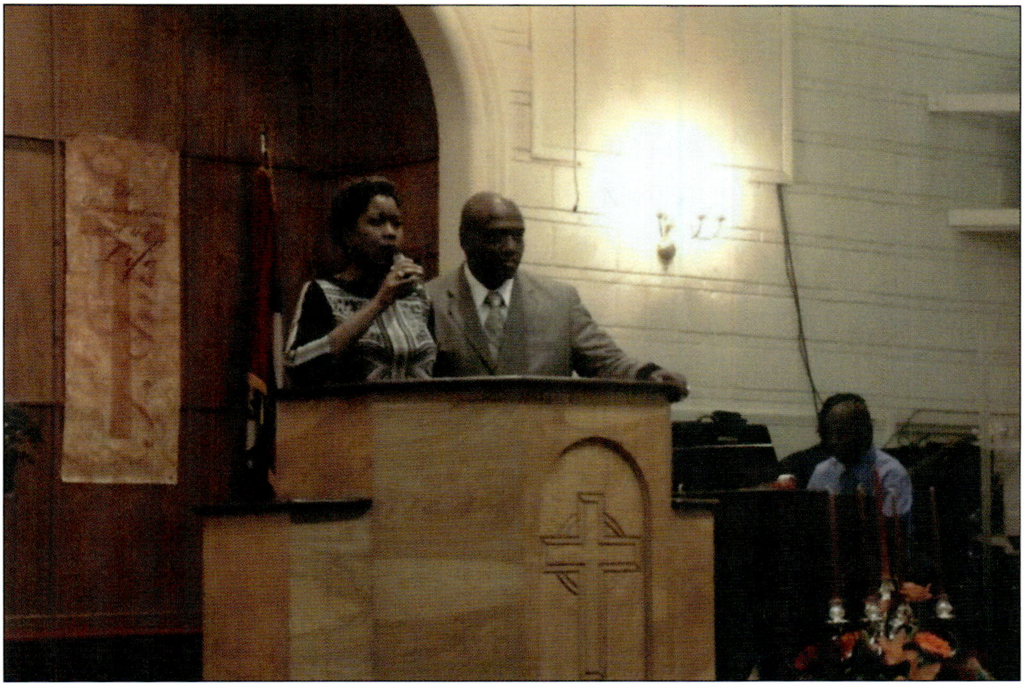

Pictured above are Lady Cynthia Bolden and Bishop James Bolden in Evangelistic Ministries Church, located at corner of Main and Elm streets. Their congregation will attest that the two are dedicated spiritual leaders. Below are Bishop Isaiah D. Thomas (front left) and Bishop James Bolden (front right) in front of the congregation. Having started their ministry in a hotel room, they grew the church to over 100 members. (Courtesy of Bishop James Bolden.)

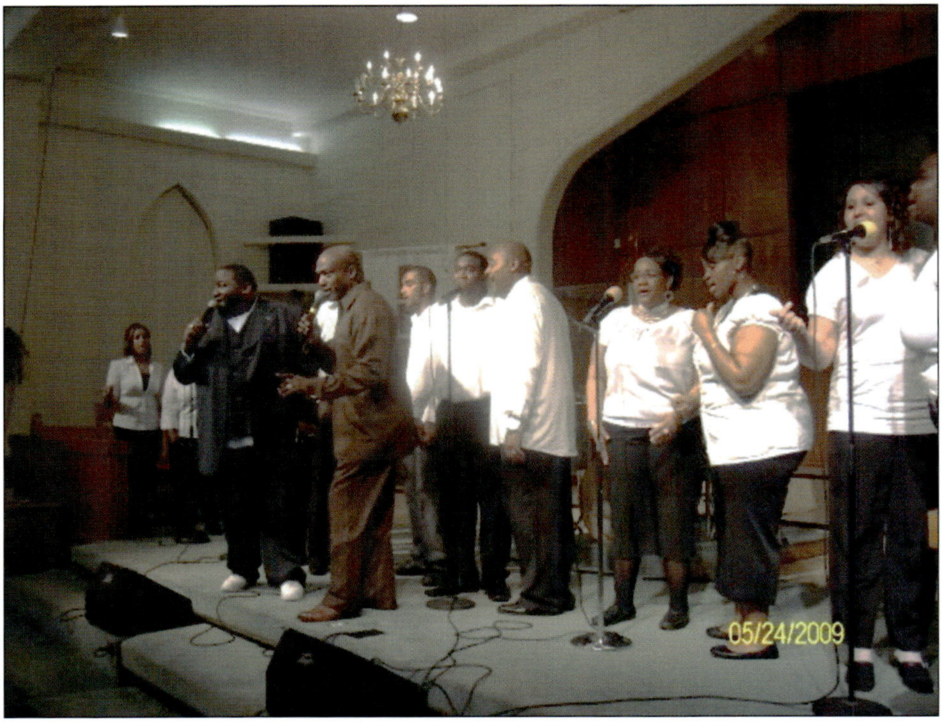

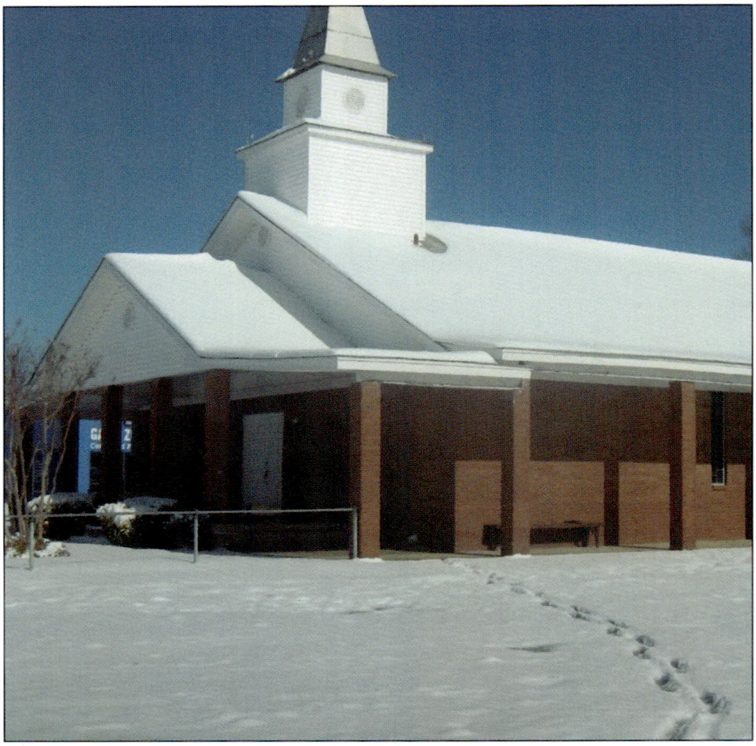

Westside Baptist Church was organized on March 8, 1959, as an arm of Temple Baptist Church in Little Rock. The pastor at this time was Br. A.J. DeVore. The church is located at 417 Dupree Drive, and the current pastor is Br. Ronnie Johnson. (Courtesy of the Jacksonville Historical District.)

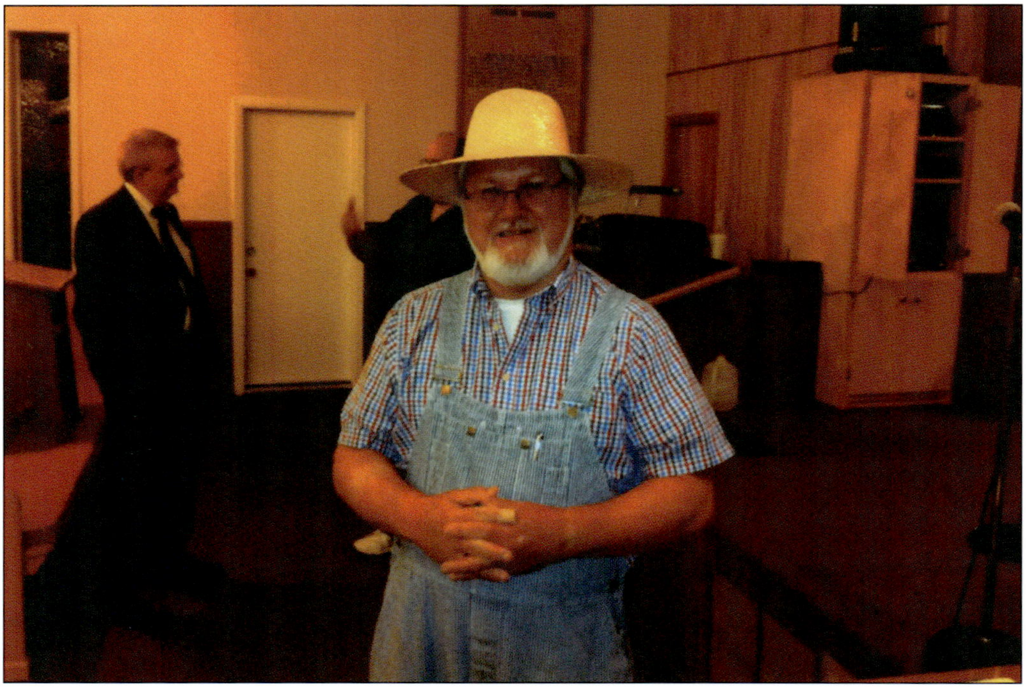

Pastor Ronnie Johnson is pictured here inside Westside Baptist Church, which has the motto, "The end of your search for a friendly church." Johnson demonstrates how to have fun with friends at church during a day with fellow Christians, enjoying food, fun, and singing at one of their annual Old Fashion Revivals. (Courtesy of Westside Baptist Church.)

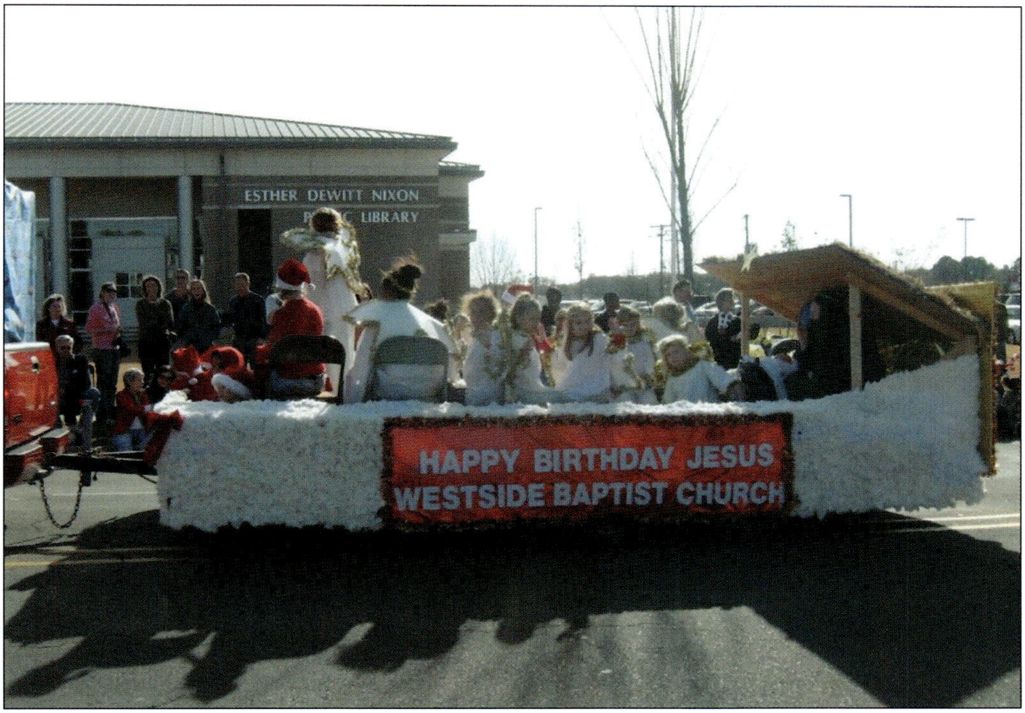

This float was made by members of Westside Baptist Church for the 2012 Christmas Parade; the theme was the birth of Christ. This float took first place in the parade. (Courtesy of Westside Baptist Church.)

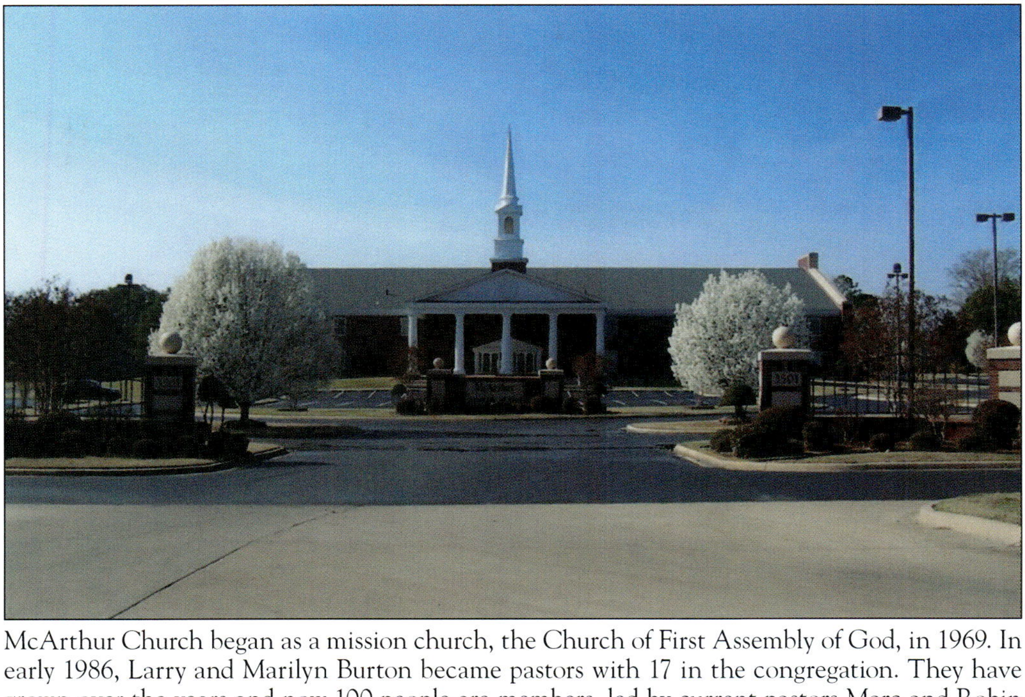

McArthur Church began as a mission church, the Church of First Assembly of God, in 1969. In early 1986, Larry and Marilyn Burton became pastors with 17 in the congregation. They have grown over the years and now 100 people are members, led by current pastors Marc and Robin Bateman. (Courtesy of the Jacksonville Historical District.)

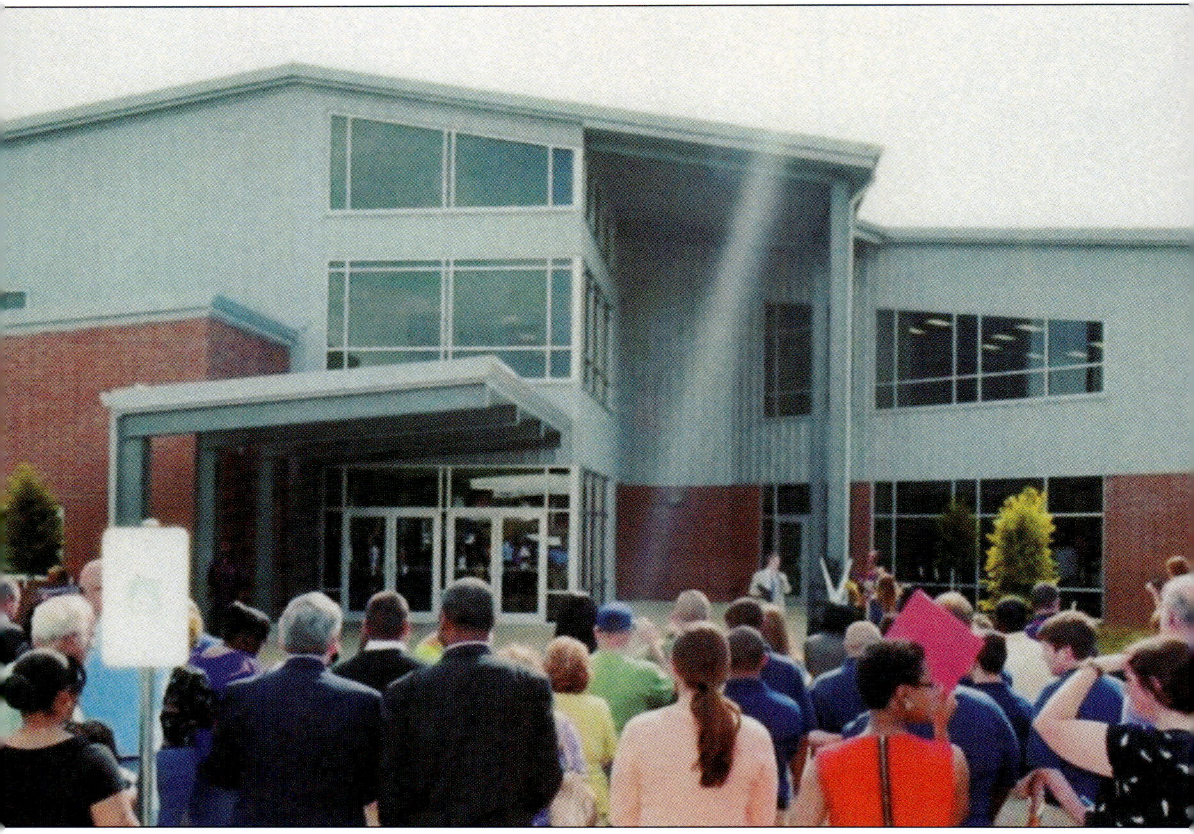

Lighthouse College Prep Academy High School was built in front of the charter school's First Street campus in Jacksonville. As of this writing, 75 ninth-graders are being housed in a temporary building for the 2015–2016 school year. One grade will be added each year until the school graduates its first class in 2017. (Courtesy of Sarah Campbell.)

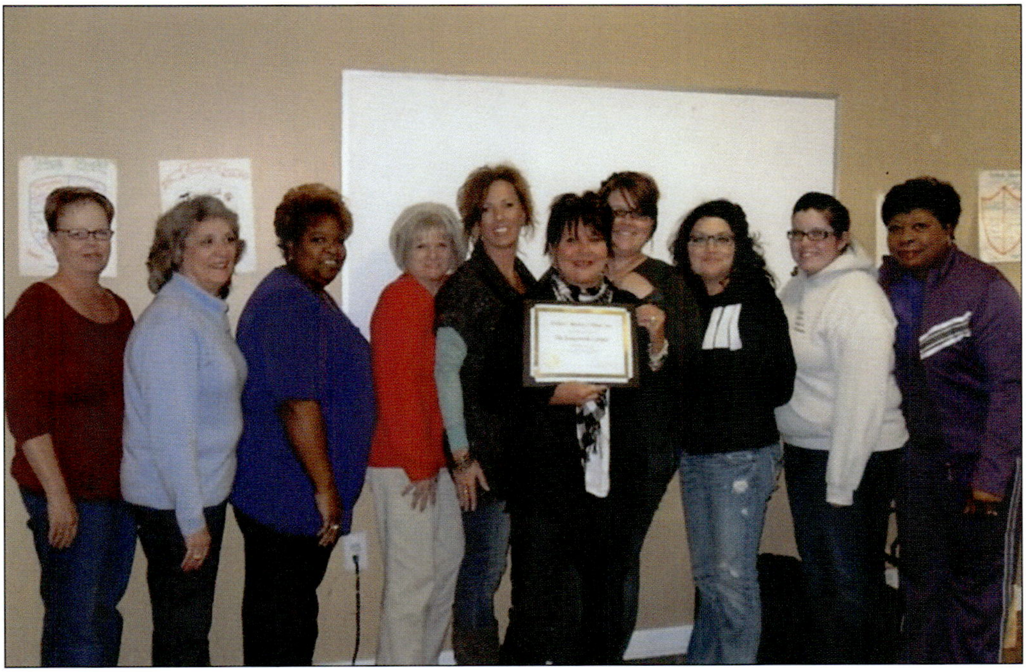

Arthurs Beauty College opened in 1971 and has been in same location for 25 years, at 2600 John Harden Drive. The current CEO and director is Chris Strawn. (Courtesy of the Jacksonville Historical District.)

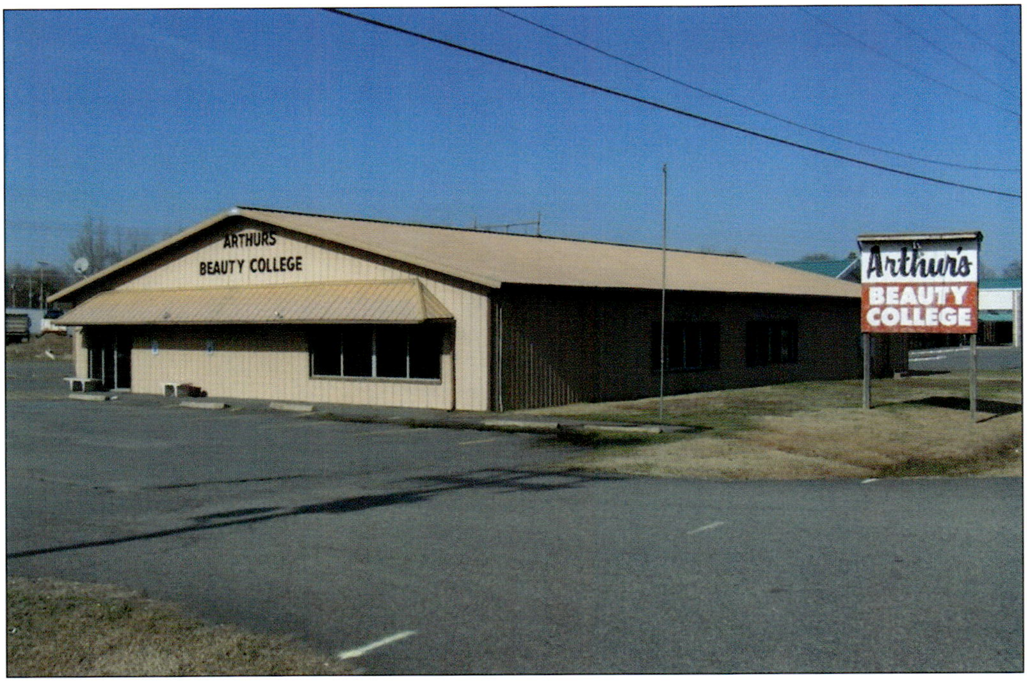

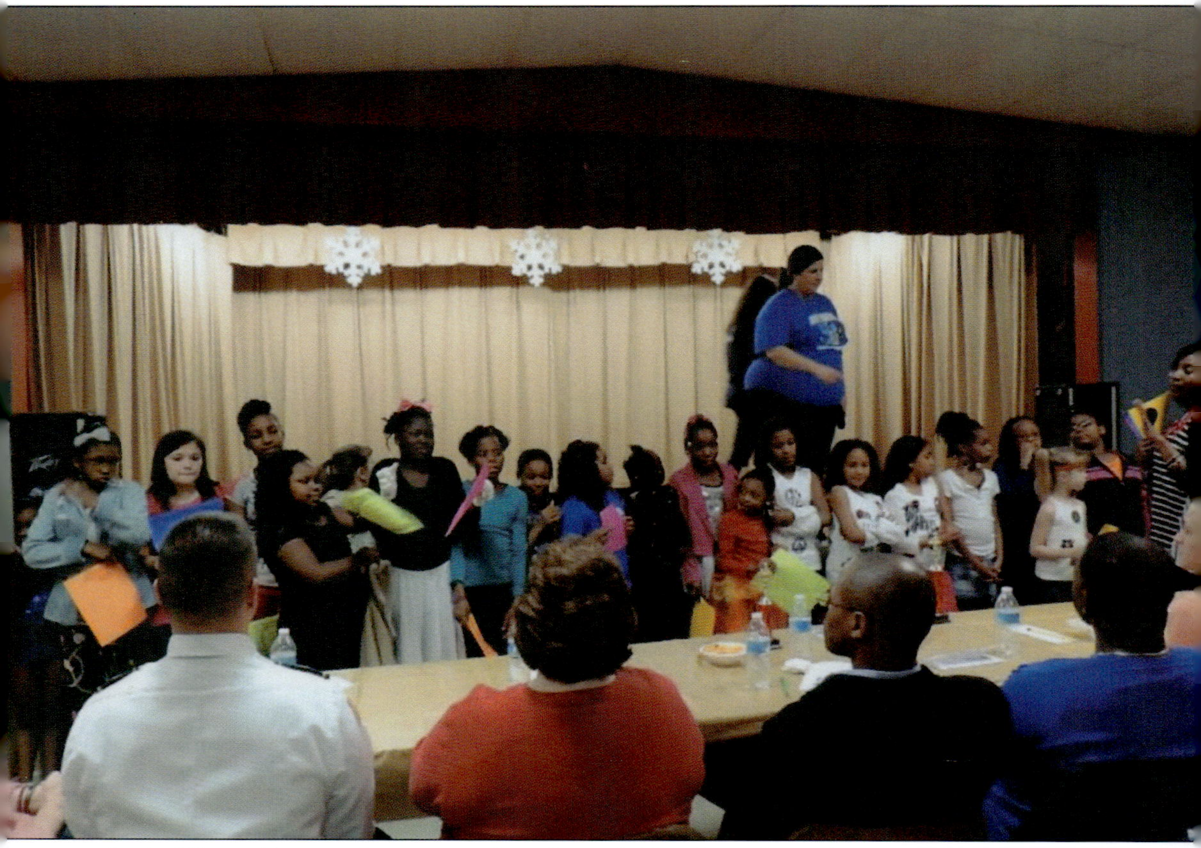

At the Warren Dupree Elementary talent show, children have fun and compete for trophies. This school was named after one of Jacksonville's forefathers, Warren Dupree. It serves students from kindergarten through the fifth grade. (Courtesy of Warren Dupree Elementary.)

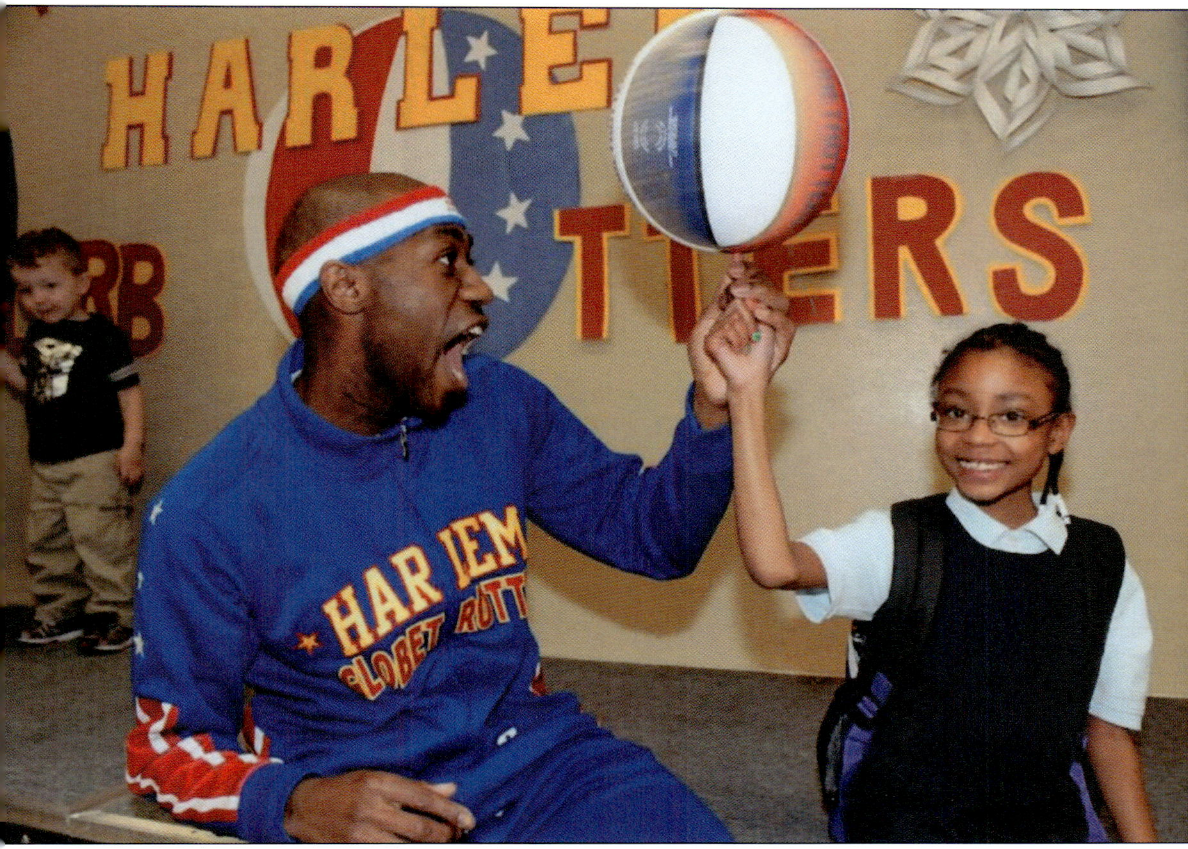

During a visit by the Harlem Globetrotters to Pathfinder Lighthouse Charter School, first-grader Camryn Williams spins a basketball on her finger with Globetrotter Tay "Firefly" Fisher. She said it was magical day. (Courtesy of the *Leader*.)

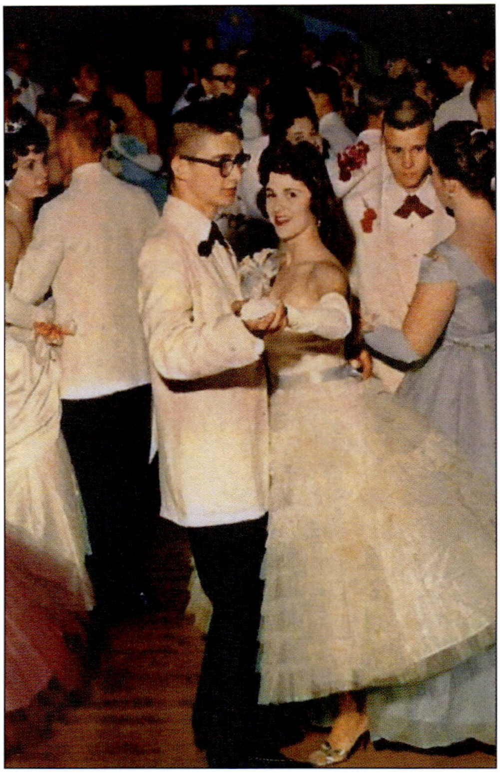

Pictured is the Jacksonville High School Prom for the class of 1967. Jacksonville High School serves 9th- through 12th-grade students in the city. This photograph illustrates the difference that 47 years makes in terms of style—but, trends always seem to come back around. (Courtesy of Jacksonville High School.)

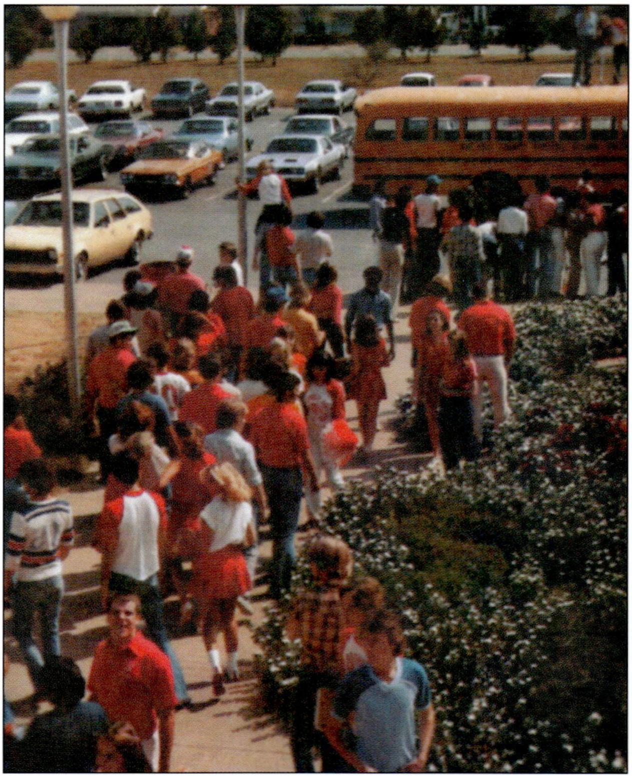

Students are pictured here on the campus of Jacksonville High School in the 1980s. This photograph provides a glimpse at what an average day looked like. (Courtesy of Wanda Sanders.)

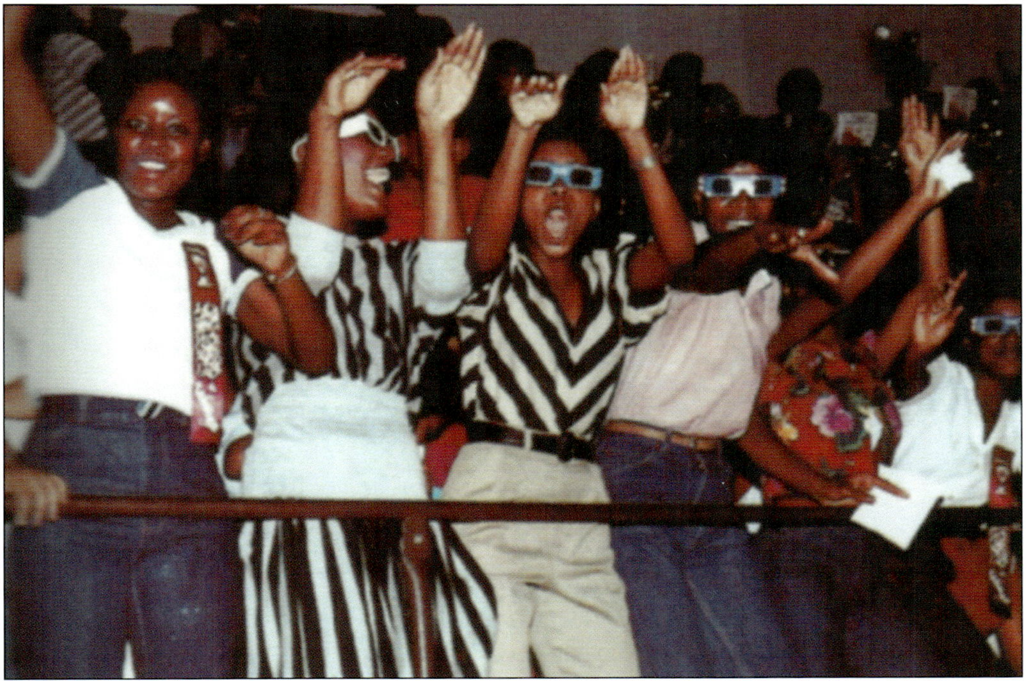

Students cheer for the Red Devils Basketball team at Jacksonville High School during a pep rally in the 1980s. There are always rallies to energize students and players for games at the school, headed by the cheerleaders, who are a driving force. (Courtesy of Wanda Sanders.)

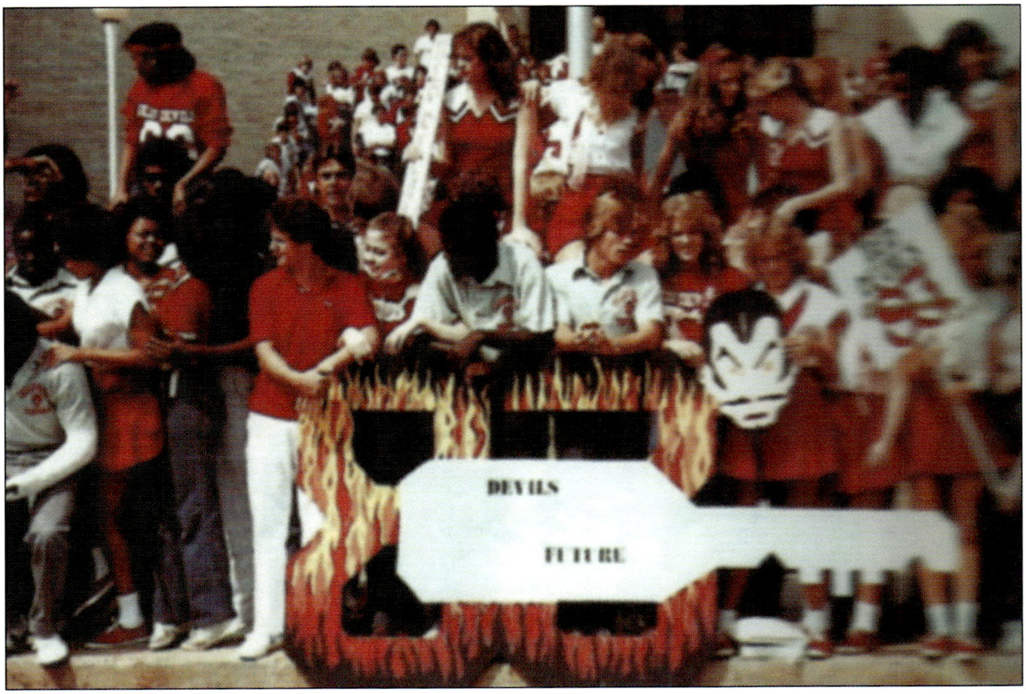

Pictured is the senior class of 1986 on the front steps at Jacksonville High School. The stairs at the high school symbolize stepping into adulthood and are the backdrop of every senior portrait. (Courtesy of Wanda Sanders.)

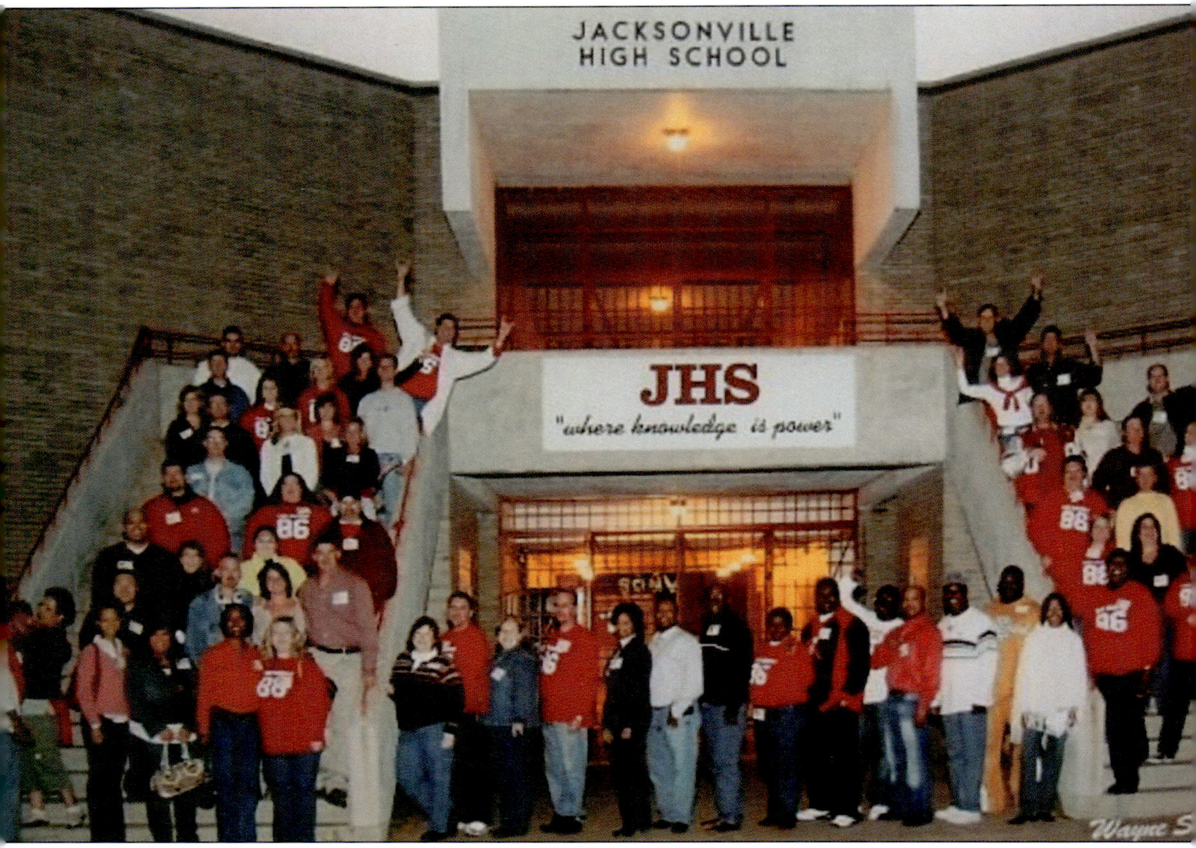

These famous Jacksonville High School stairs are in every yearbook, with the seniors standing on and in front of them. (Courtesy of the Jacksonville Historical District.)

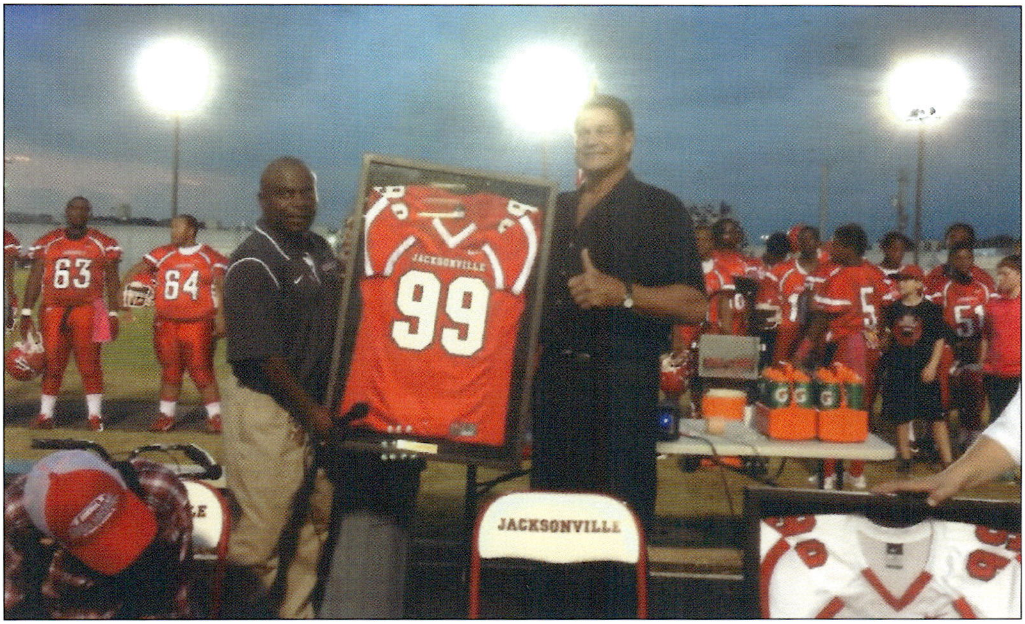

Pictured is Daniel Oliver Hampton, also known as "Danimal." Born on September 19, 1957, Hampton is a retired NFL defensive tackle who played 12 seasons for the Chicago Bears (1979 to 1990). He was elected to the Pro Football Hall of Fame in 2002. In 2014, after a 39-year wait, the most decorated athlete in Jacksonville High School history finally had his high school number retired. (Courtesy of the Jacksonville Historical District.)

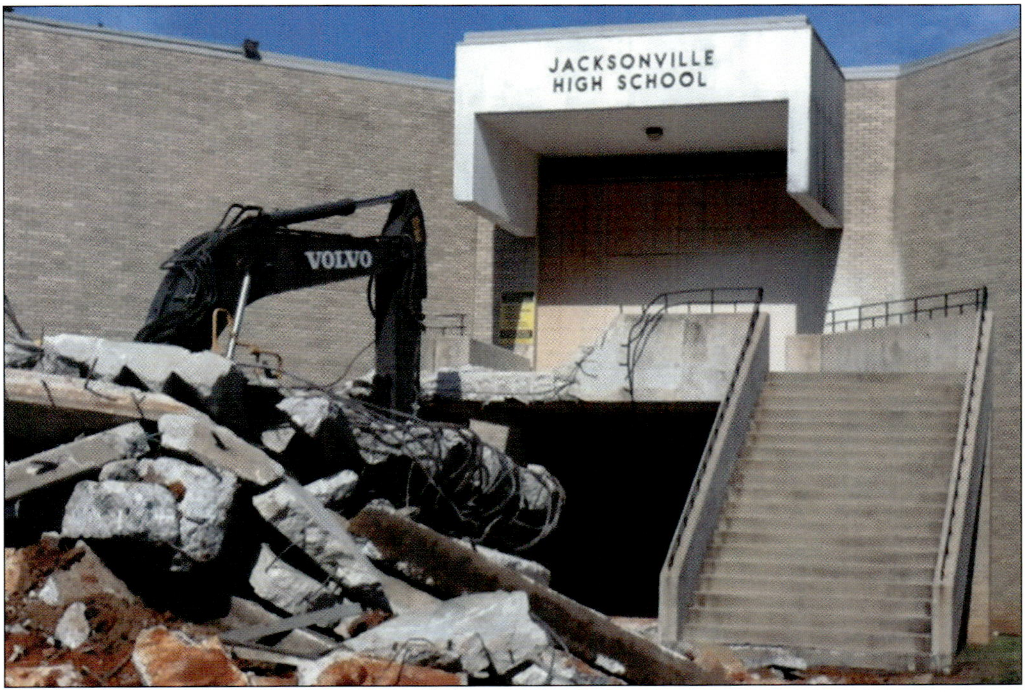

In 2013, the steps at Jacksonville High School were removed from the school's entrance because of safety issues; they were falling apart after so many years of standing tall. (Courtesy of the Jacksonville Historical District.)

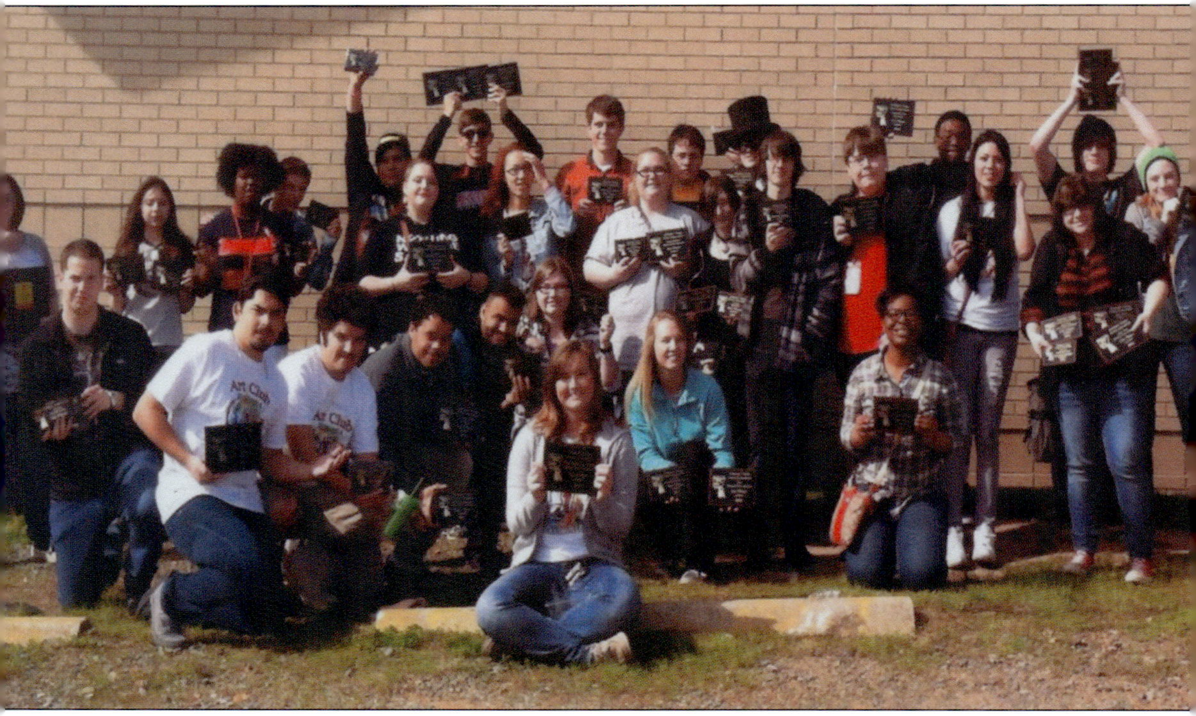

The 40 members of the Jacksonville High School Art Club attended the Arkansas Young Artist Association State Art Contest on Wednesday, April 16, 2014. Award winners pictured here include Arron Woodall, Mary Jane Hewitt, Tiffany Smith, Jouse Zarate, Chris Erkel, Charisse Russell, Thomas Brooks, Alex Williams, Nathan Hilliard, Felix Kanicke, Julissa Armenta, Keosha Banks, Blial Rasul-llah, Aston Sharp, Carmen Moody, Stephen Davis, Bryant Carter, Kayla Griffin, Zach Allen, Kaitlyn Kelly, Courtney Moody, Cheyenne Emerson, Jordon Belew, Joseph Gomez, Nikola Basheski, Tuker Felix, John Hermann, and Brianna Mashburn. Also, Nikota Basheski and Christa Gitschag won scholarship awards to Memphis College of Art. The school and community are extremely proud of these winners and the Jacksonville High School art department for all their success and accomplishments in 2014. Congratulations to them and their teachers, Glenda McCune and coach Marvin Lindley. (Courtesy of Marvin Lindley.)

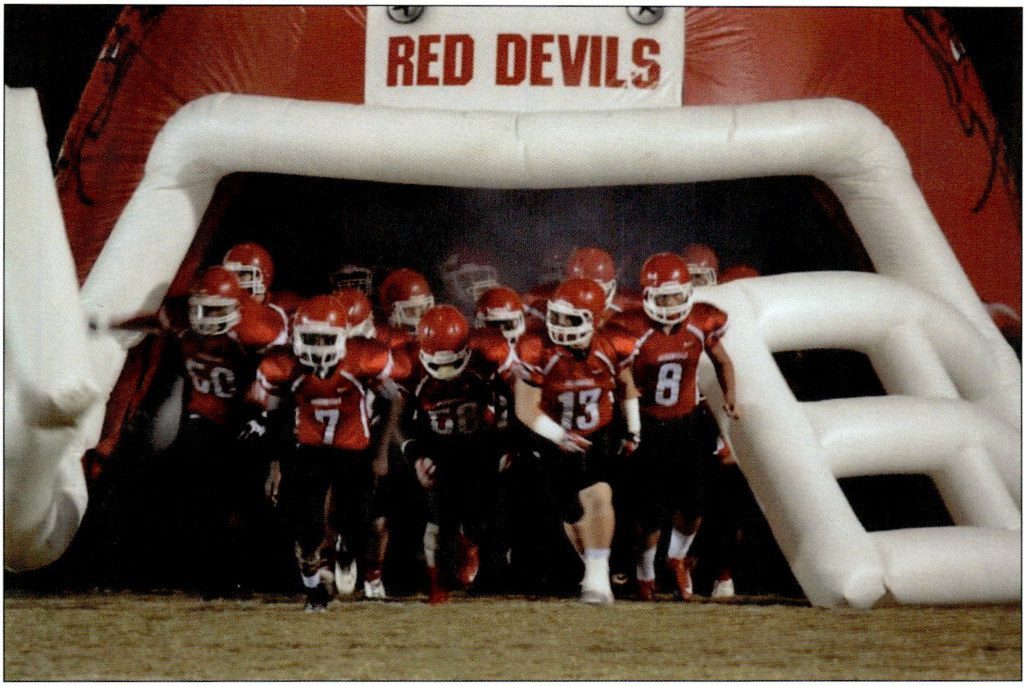

A seven-man football team of the 1930s sat together in the back of the high school classroom and sometimes caused a little trouble. Their leader was Red Brickell, and the teachers started calling that area of the classroom "Red Devils Den." The name caught on, and the team nickname changed from the Cardinals to the Red Devils; however, the school did not have an official football team until 1947. Above, the Red Devils are running out on the field at the beginning of one of their home games. Below, the football team is sitting on bleachers listening to their coach inspire them. (Courtesy of Jacksonville High School.)

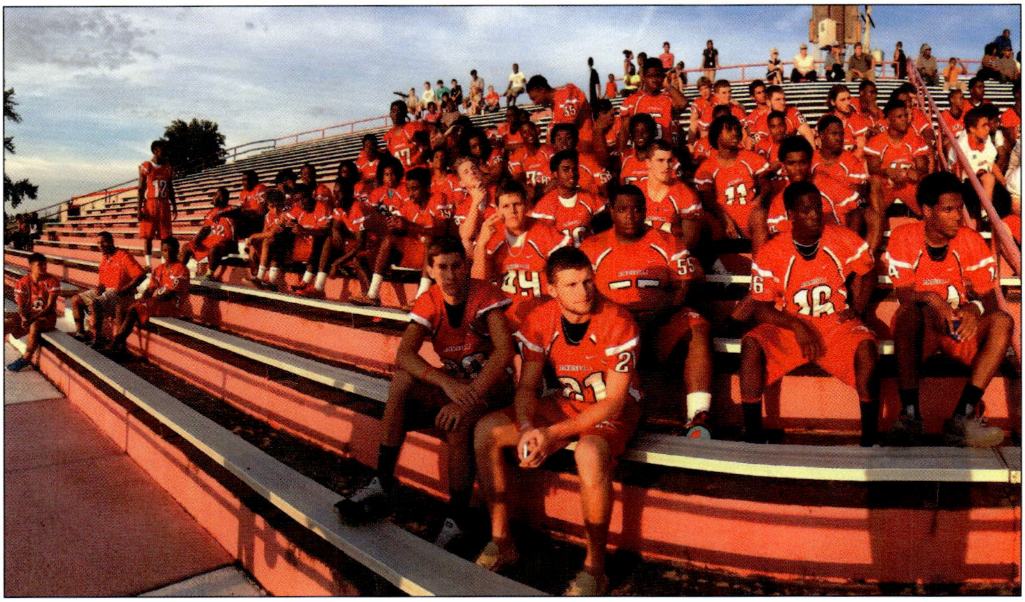

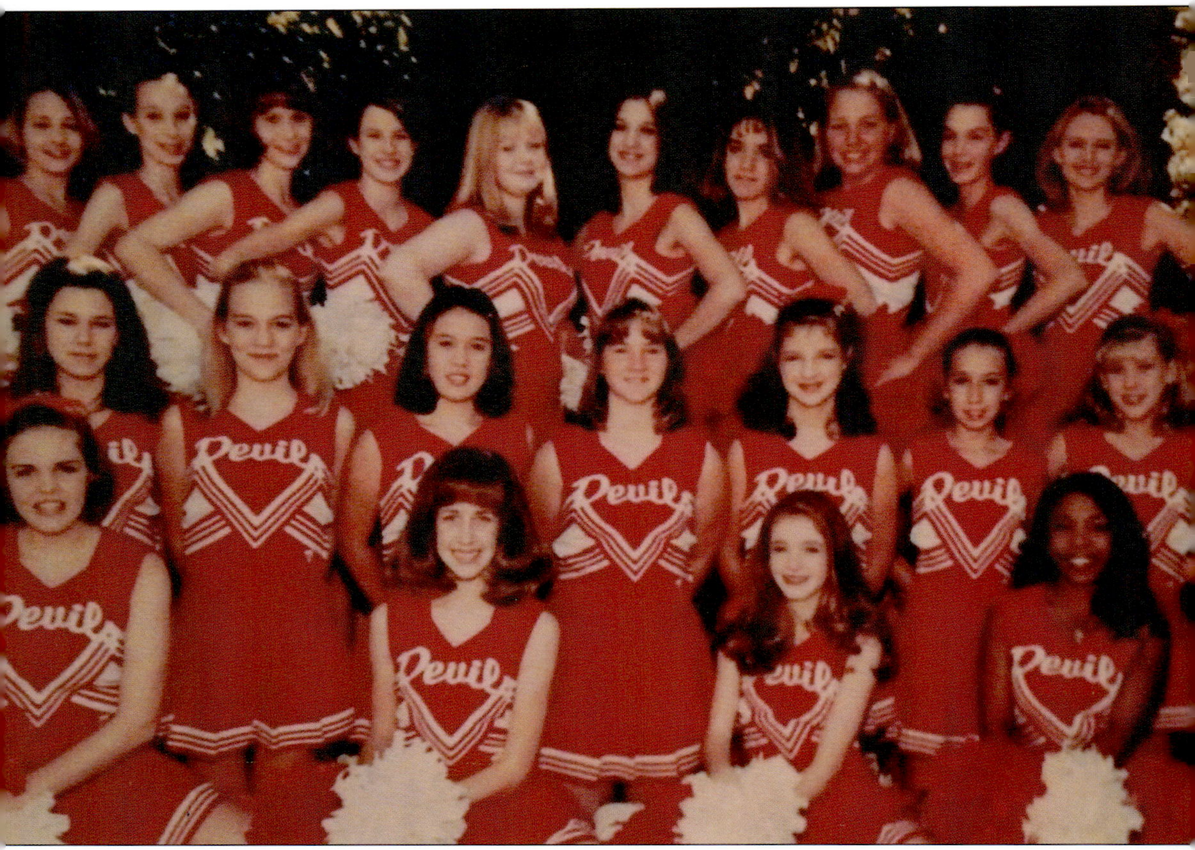

In 2000, these Red Devil cheerleaders from Jacksonville High School were as important as the football players. Together, they brought high energy to every game. (Courtesy of Niki Bolton.)

Three

Government and Public Works

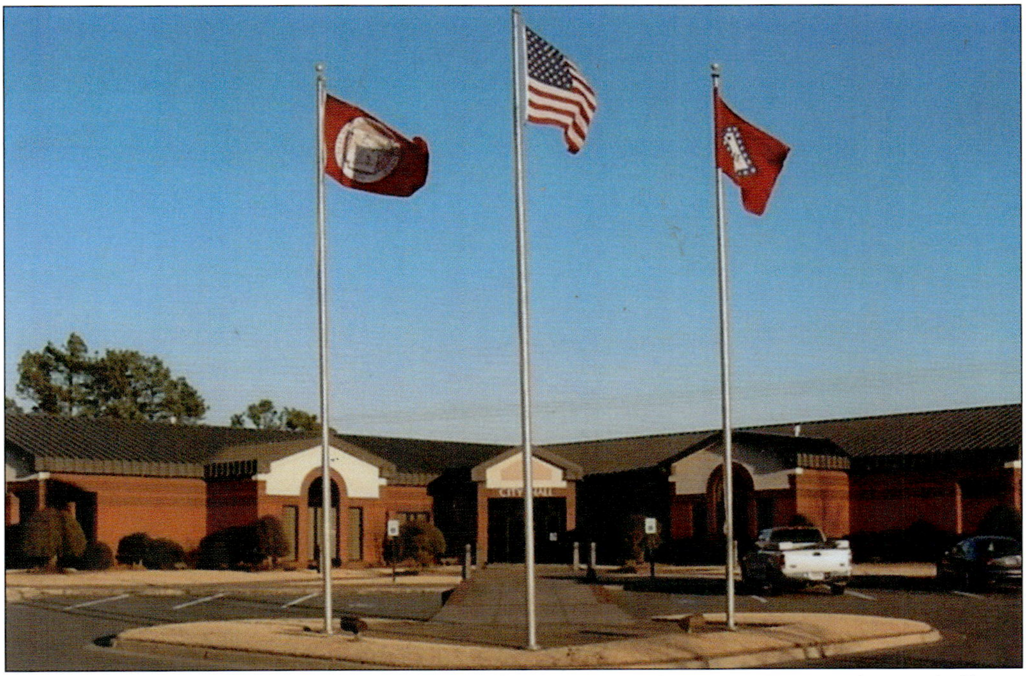

Jacksonville City Hall, located on 1 Municipal Drive, opened in 1990. Previously, city hall was situated at 109 South Second Street. In the last 75 years, Jacksonville has had 12 different men elected as mayor. They are, in chronological order, J.H. Bailey (1941–1942), P.W. Dupree Jr. (1942), Dr. C.H. Hudson (1943–1945), John E. Croft (1946–1947), Carl Brewer (1948–1951), W.F. Cramer (1952), W.W. Keaton (1953–1954), Edward D. Schmitt (1955–1960), Johns H. Harden (1961–1974), James G. Reid (1975–1986), Tommy Swaim (1986–2009), and Gary Fletcher (2009 to present). (Courtesy of Jill Ross.)

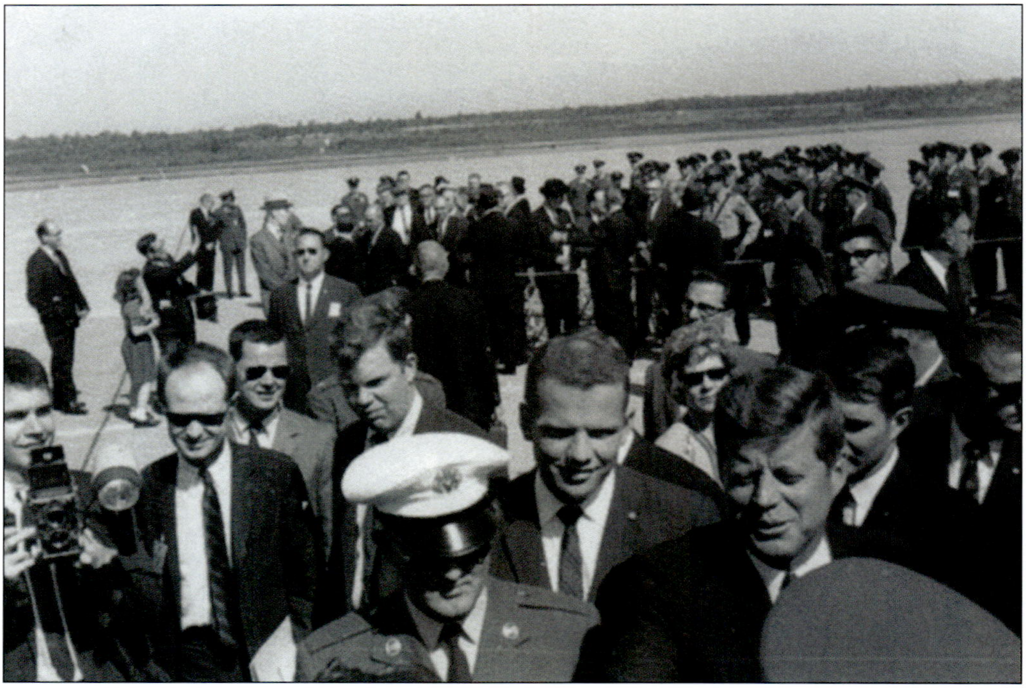

Pres. John F. Kennedy visited Little Rock Air Force Base on October 3, 1963, one month and 19 days before his death. He stopped here while on his way to dedicate Greers Ferry Dam in Heber Springs, Arkansas. (Courtesy of Little Rock Air Force Base.)

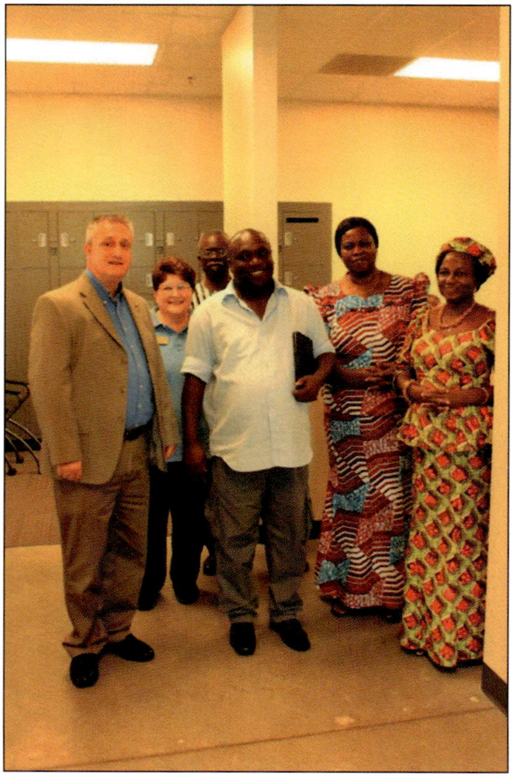

This group posing for the camera is taking part in the Sister Cities International program. From left to right, Lt. Dean Scroggins and Ald. Barbara Mashburn welcomed to the city the honorable mayor of KpandoTogbe, Dagadu VIII; paramount king of the Kpando Municipality, James Kofi Fonu Kpatakpa; youth leader of Kpando Municipal Assembly, Paulina Delali Adinyria; and queen mother of Kpando, Mama Komla Teng II. (Courtesy of the Jacksonville Police Department.)

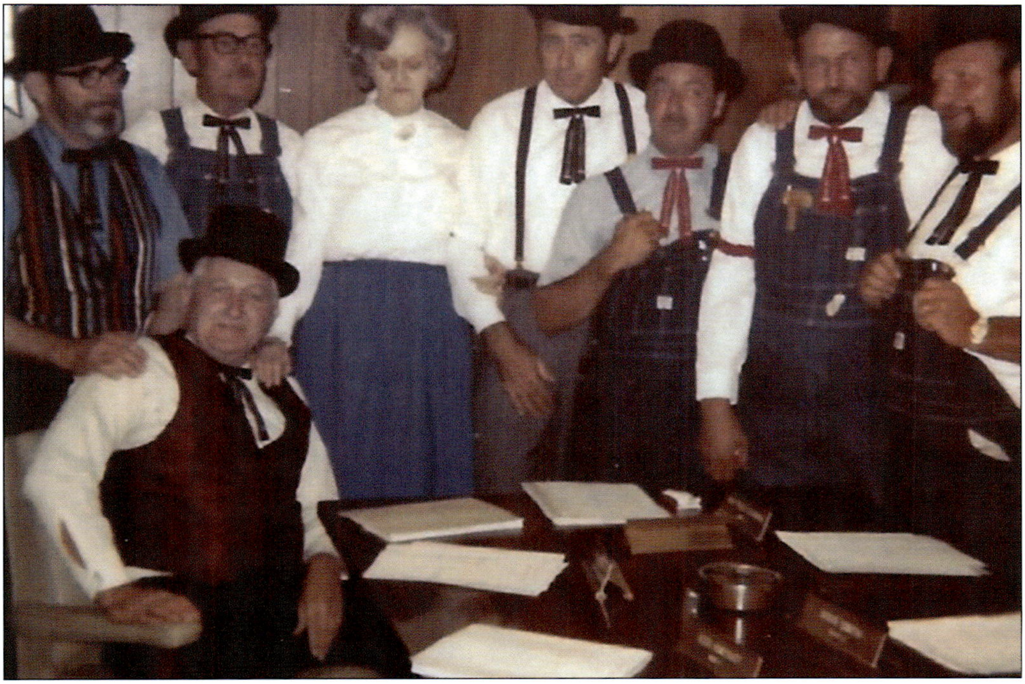

On June 23, 1970, city officials dressed up as they would have a century ago. Pictured here are, from left to right, Osco Honeycutt (alderman), Leon Sorrels (alderman), Floy Bonnie Avants (city clerk), Bill Alberson (alderman), Doug Smith (alderman), Bill Lehman (alderman), and Bob Hill (alderman), with Mayor John Harden sitting in the chair. (Courtesy of Susan Davitt.)

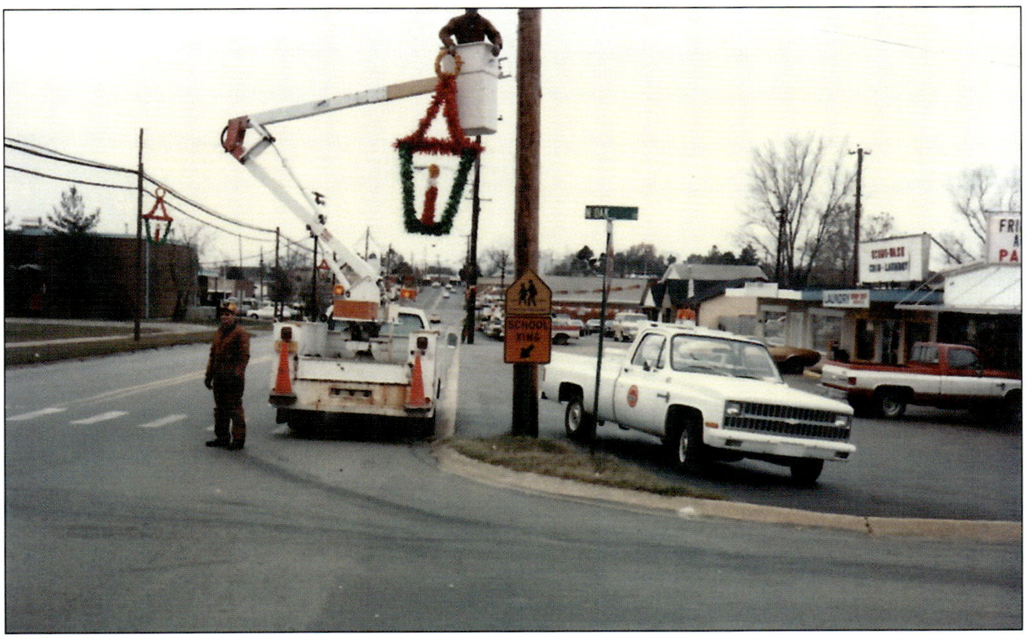

A Jacksonville street worker puts up Christmas decorations on a light pole. This is done annually around December 1, before the Christmas parade on the first Saturday of the month. (Courtesy of the Jacksonville Public Works Department.)

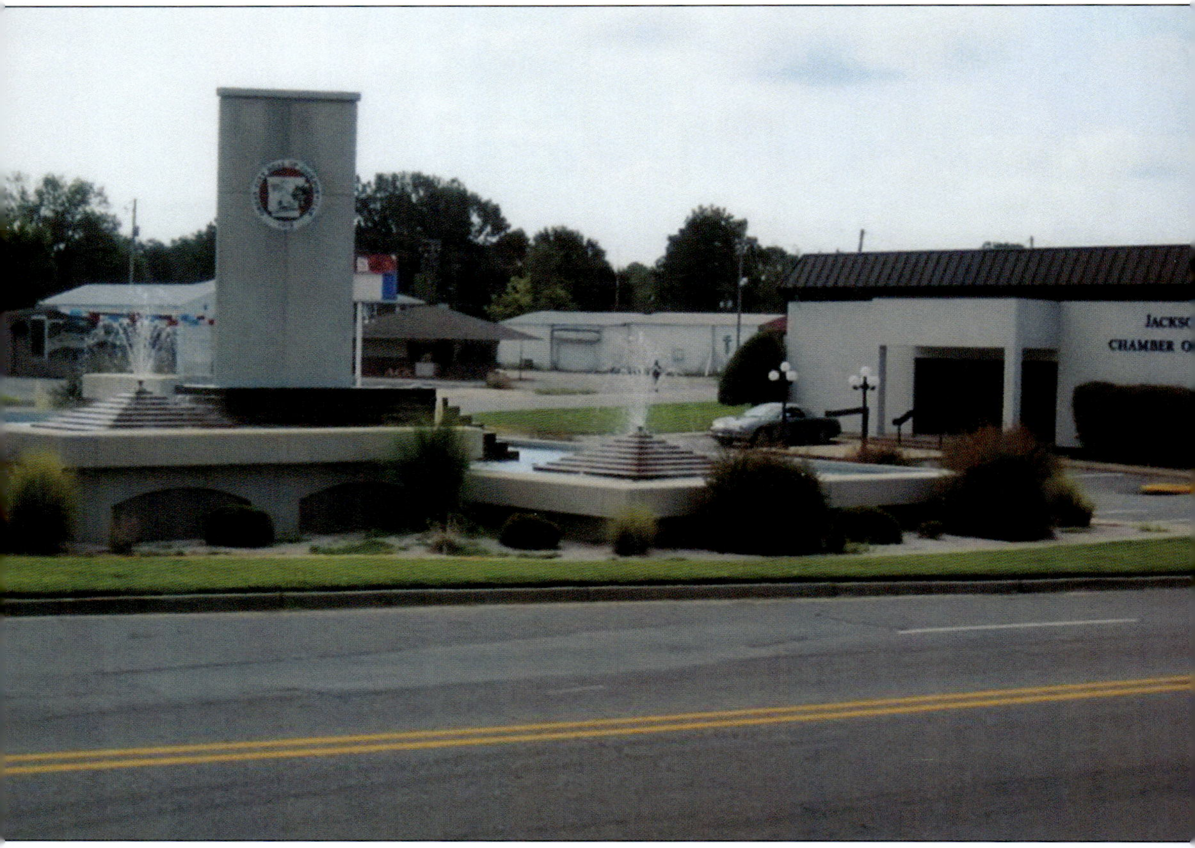

The charter for the Jacksonville Chamber of Commerce was filed on November 28, 1947. The purpose was to build and maintain the economic security of the area. Establishment of a bank headed the list of objectives of the first meeting. In addition to the bank, the program of activity mapped by the group was to advertise the area as an industrial site and secure industries, develop roads and streets, public utilities, and sanitation and establish city zoning and building codes. The officers were Kenneth Pat Wilson (president), Ed Shultz (vice president), Joe Hudson (secretary), and Fred Bowen (treasurer). The original building for the chamber of commerce was located at 1400 West Main Street and purchased for $27.50 per square foot. The second building, which currently houses the chamber of commerce, is located at 200 Dupree Drive, procured in agreement with Mayor James Reid on November 16, 1978. (Courtesy of the Jacksonville Historical District.)

Jacksonville firefighters are pictured here in full gear, which they wear to protect themselves from fire and smoke as they work. (Courtesy of the Jacksonville Fire Department.)

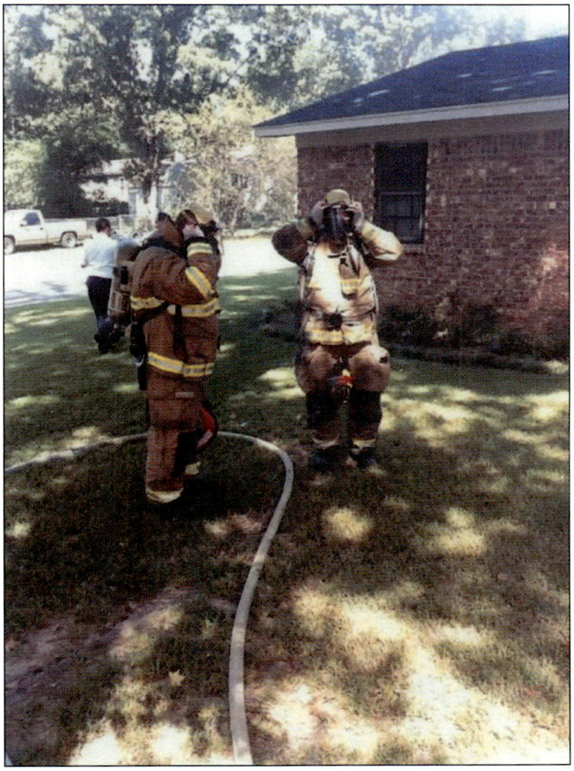

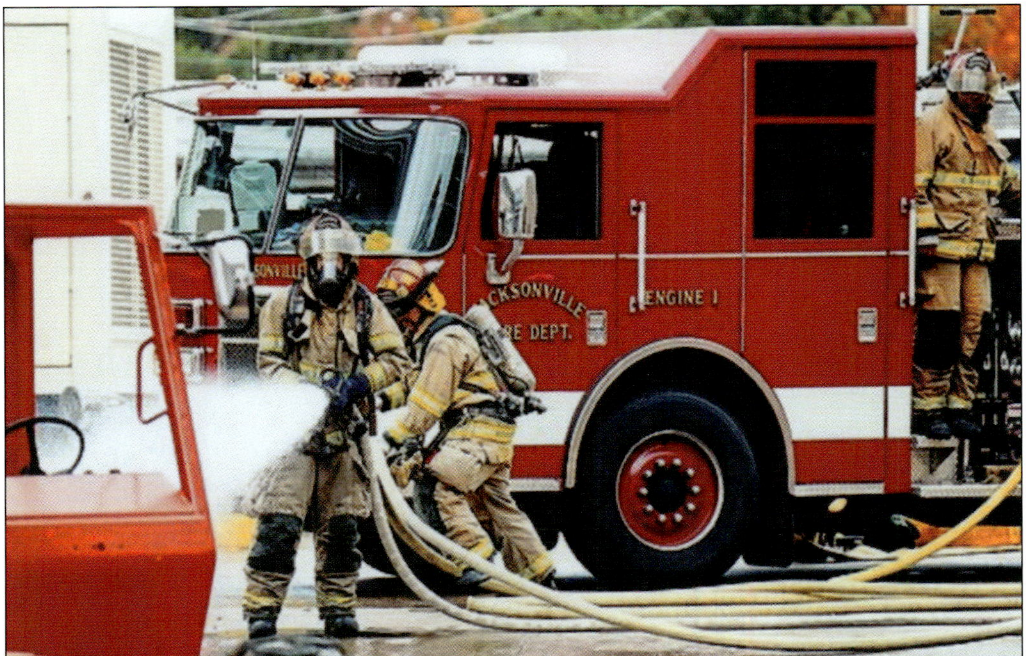

Employees of Ashland Performance Materials in Jacksonville are keeping their emergency-preparedness skills on point, thanks to an annual emergency drill, which they have been performing since 1949. (Courtesy of the Jacksonville Fire Department.)

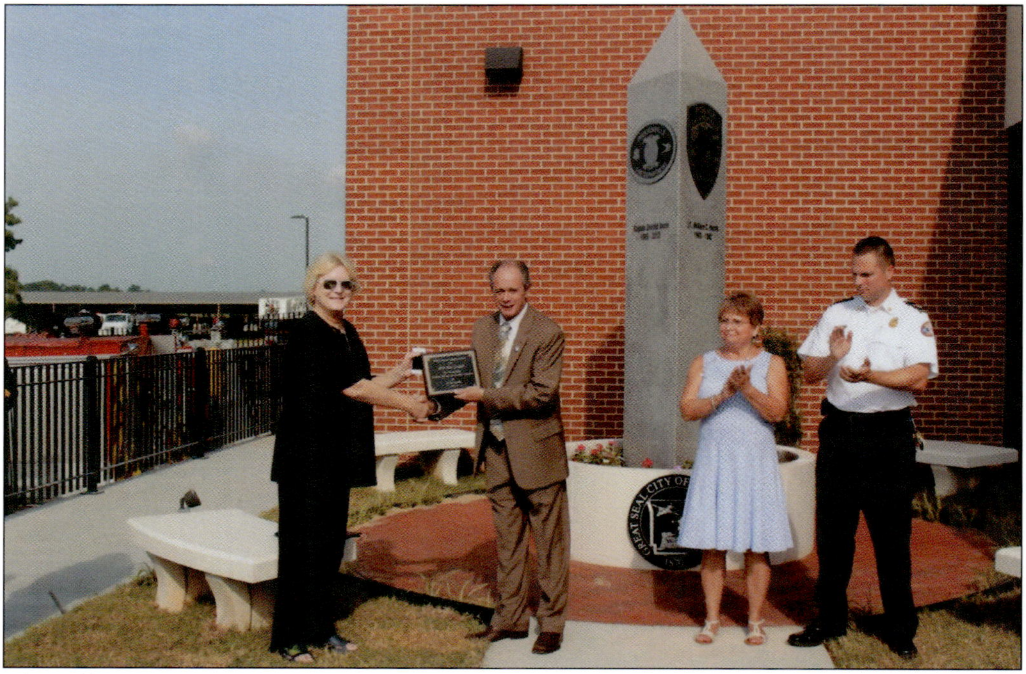

The Fallen Heroes Memorial was built for Jacksonville's heroes killed in the line of duty. It was dedicated in March 2014. Pictured here are, from left to right, local artist and designer of the memorial RB McGrath, Mayor Gary Fletcher, Betty Jones (widow of fire department captain Donald Jones), and fire chief Alan Laughy. The idea behind this memorial came from author Ald. Barbara Mashburn, who wanted a way to help the city remember fallen firefighters and police officers. (Courtesy of Sarah Campbell.)

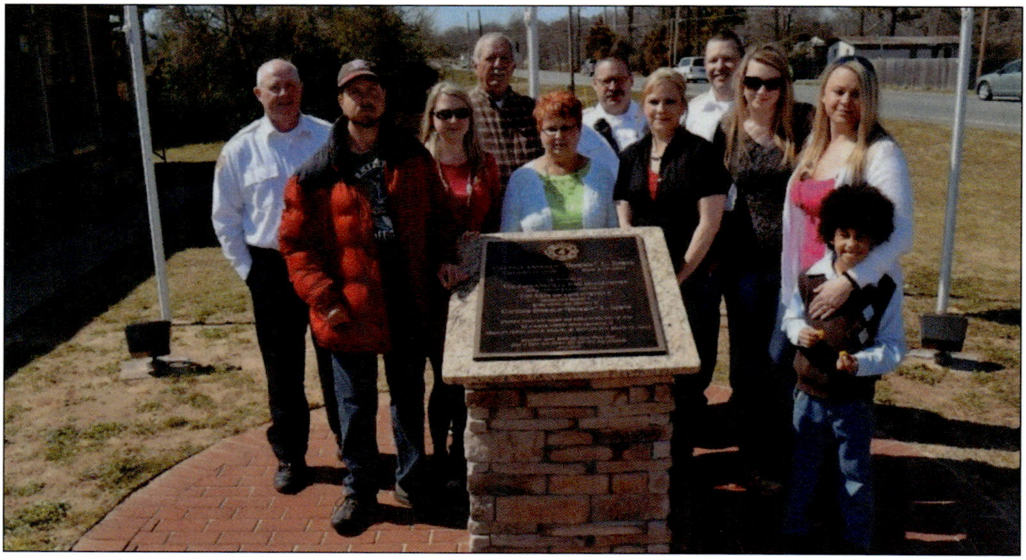

Family and friends of Capt. Donald "Donnie" Jones attend the 2013 memorial dedication of Fire Station Four on Highway 161. Jones was killed in the line of duty in March 2012. From left to right are battalion chief Bob Thornton, Vernon Myers Jr., Beverly Smiley, retired chief John Vanderhoof, Betty Jones, battalion chief Eddie Hill, Donna Henderson, battalion chief Joe Bratton, Tori Henderson, Teresa Myers, and Ali Sanders. (Courtesy of Sarah Campbell.)

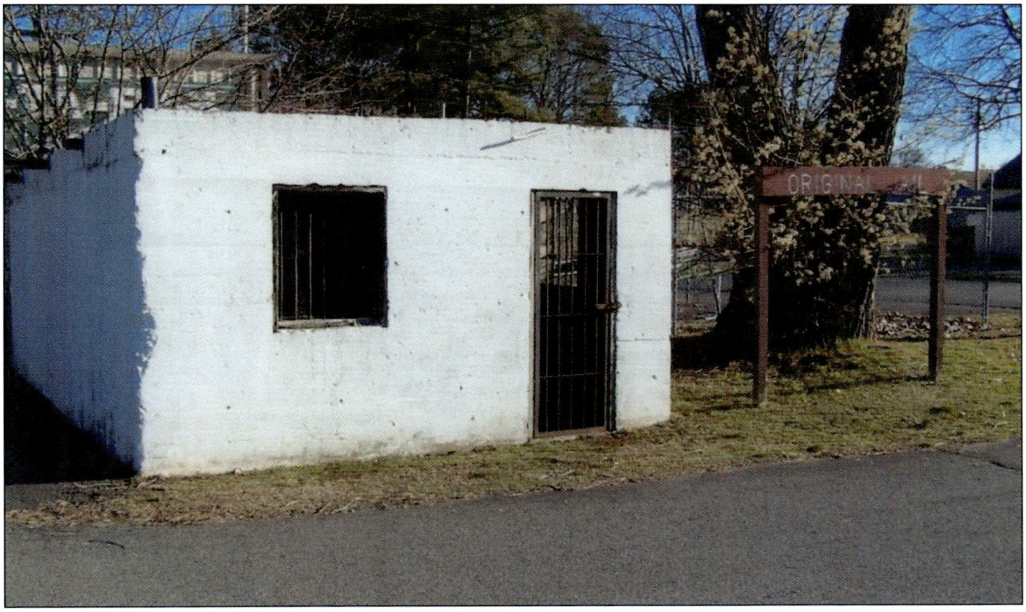

Old City Jail, at 408 East Center Street, opened in 1943 for petty crooks and rowdy drunks. According to Marshal Buddy Crook, "It got cold in there, but if they'd do right, they didn't get in there." The facility had two cells with doors, two iron beds, and a wood-burning stove in the corner (but with barred windows, it did little to keep out the cold). The jail closed in 1952, and it is being considered for the National Register of Historic Places. (Courtesy of the Jacksonville Historical District.)

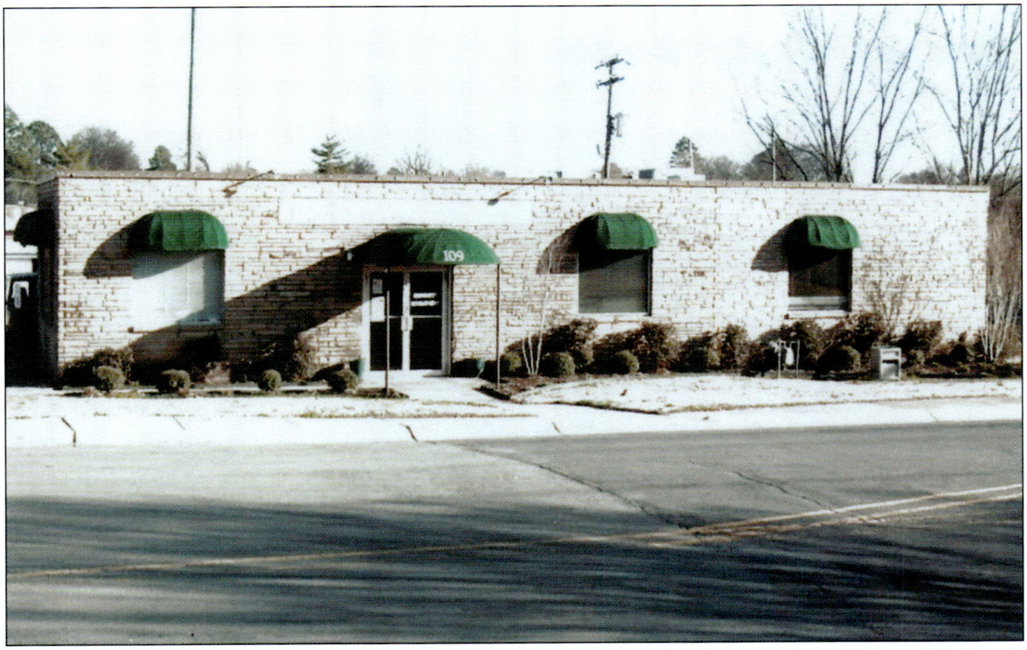

This is the police and courts building, or municipal building, which opened in 1952 at 109 South Second Street under Marshal Clarence Garner (marshal from 1946 to 1956) and Mayor W.F. Cramer. This facility closed in 1956 when a new building was opened on Main Street. (Courtesy of the Jacksonville Historical District.)

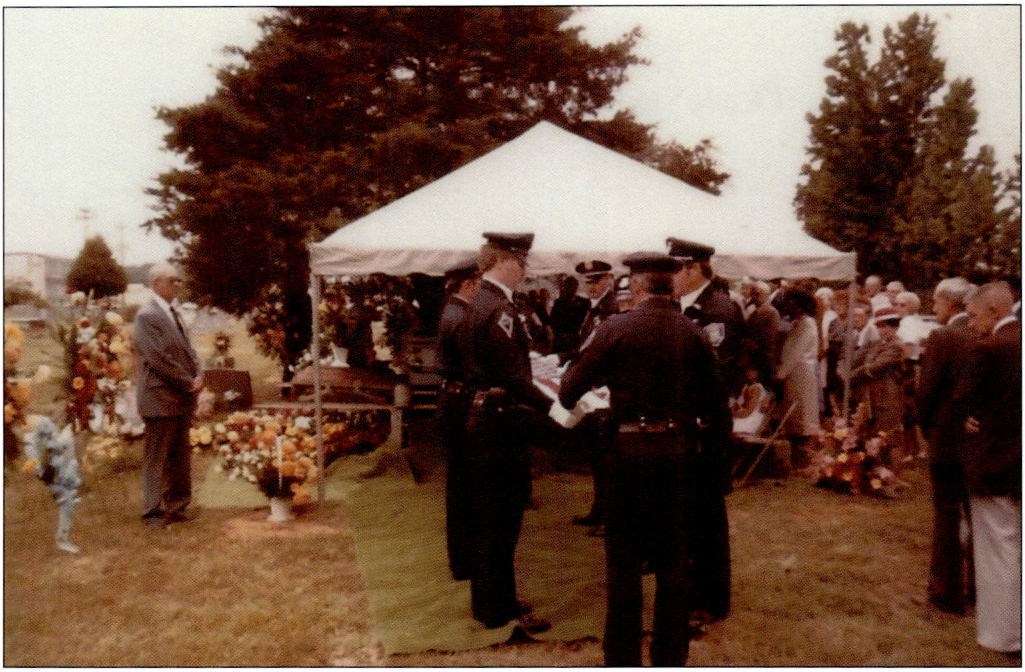

Above is the funeral of William Harris, a Jacksonville police officer for 19 years who died at age of 59. His name is on the Fallen Heroes Memorial Wall. Below are the officers who attended Harris's funeral. From left to right are (first row) Larry Hibbs, Kenneth Bouillon, Bennie Tolbert, and Frank Neely; (second row) Donald Egelhoff, David Bjork, Jim Lewis, Charles Reshel, and James Walther. (Above, courtesy of the City of Jacksonville; below, courtesy of the Jacksonville Police Department.)

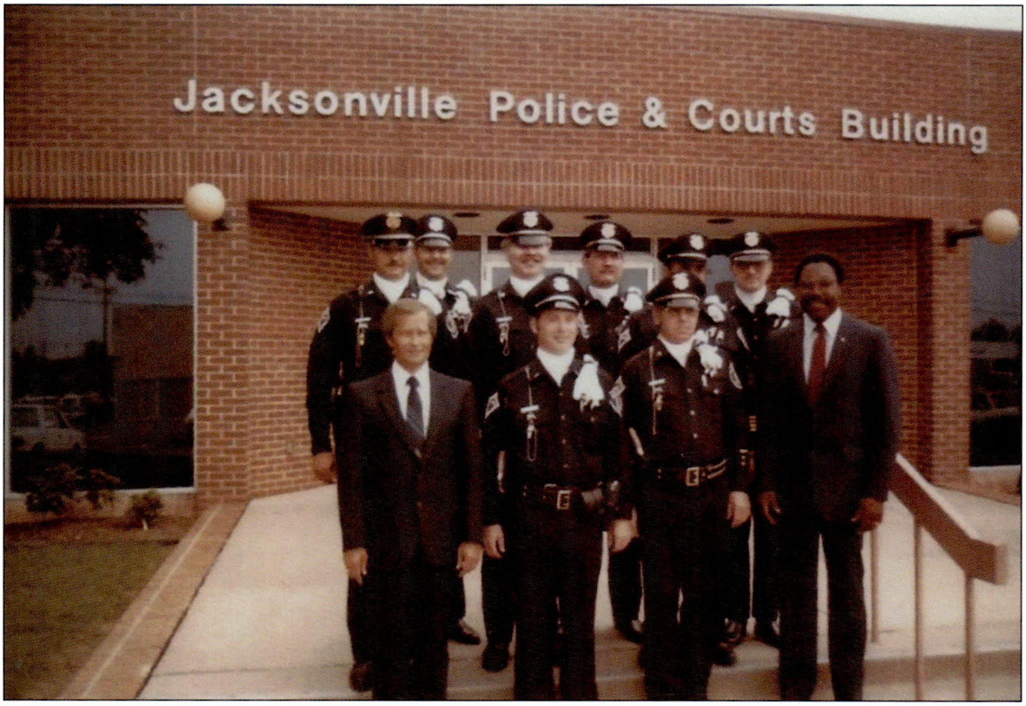

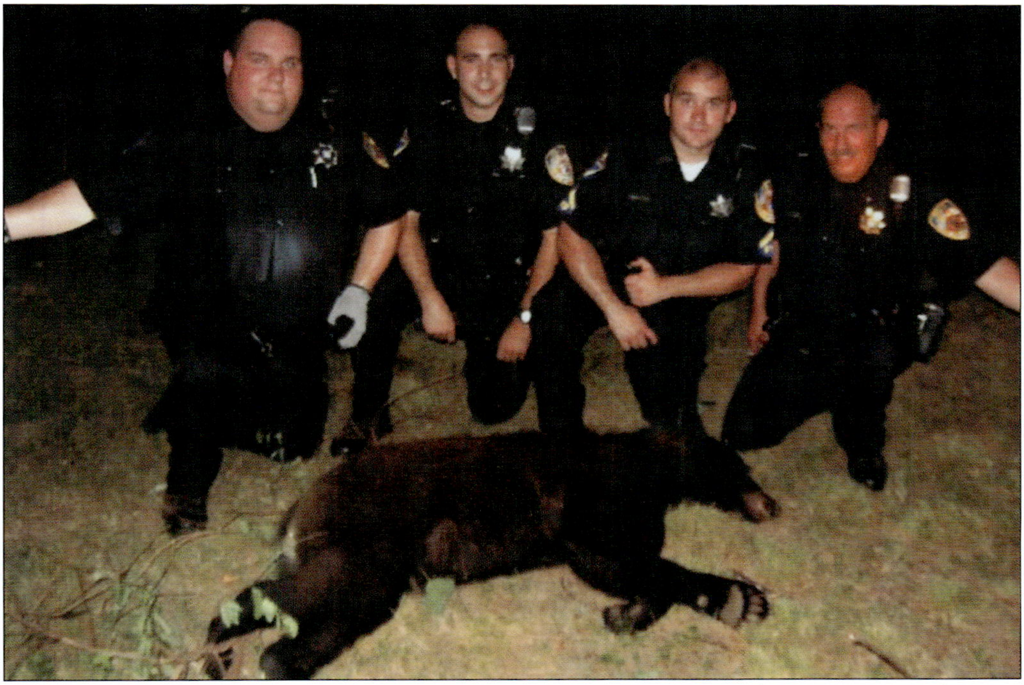

From left to right, Officer Waymack, Officer Portale, Officer Evans, and Lieutenant Mayberry of the Jacksonville Police Department have tranquilized this black bear on North James Street. The bear was relocated by the Arkansas Game and Fish Commission. (Courtesy of the Jacksonville Police Department.)

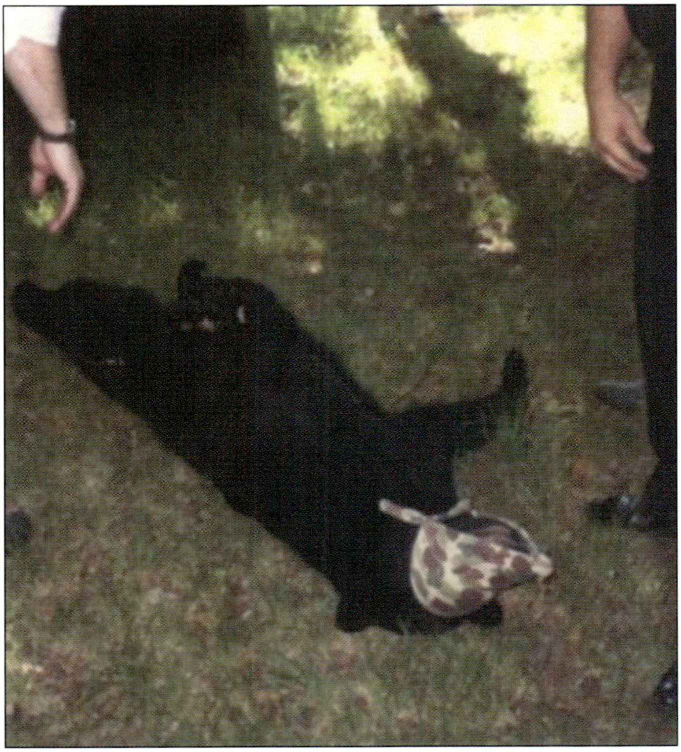

The tranquilized 300-pound black bear is seen before being relocated. (Courtesy of the Jacksonville Police Department.)

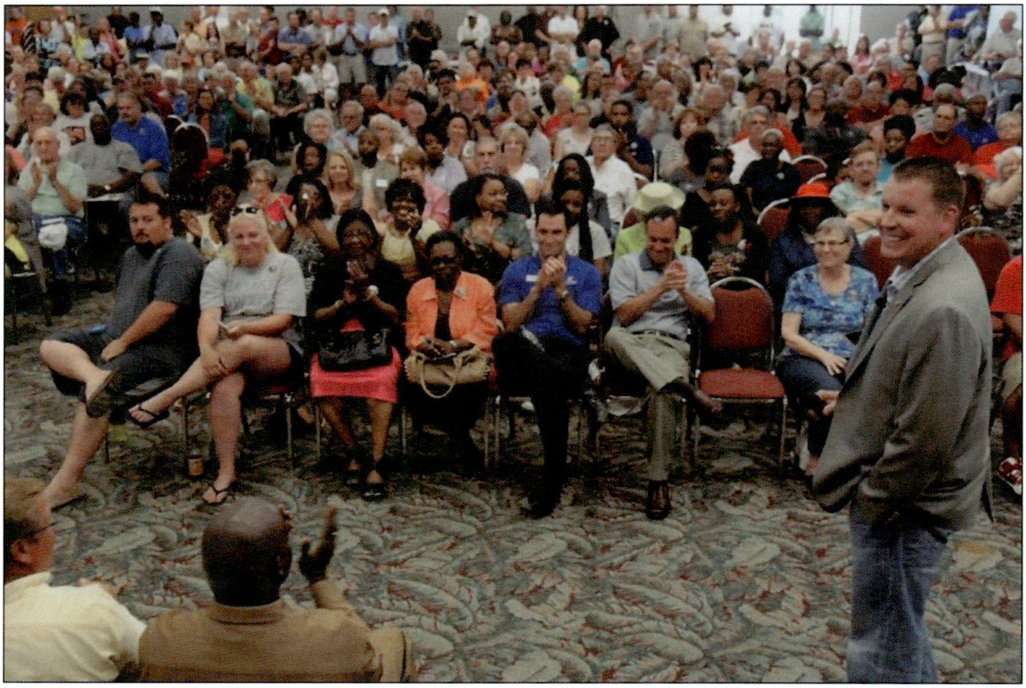

A great day for Jacksonville is captured here by the camera; this photograph was taken right before the town voted unanimously to have its own school district. The man standing is Daniel Gray, president of the school board. (Courtesy of the City of Jacksonville.)

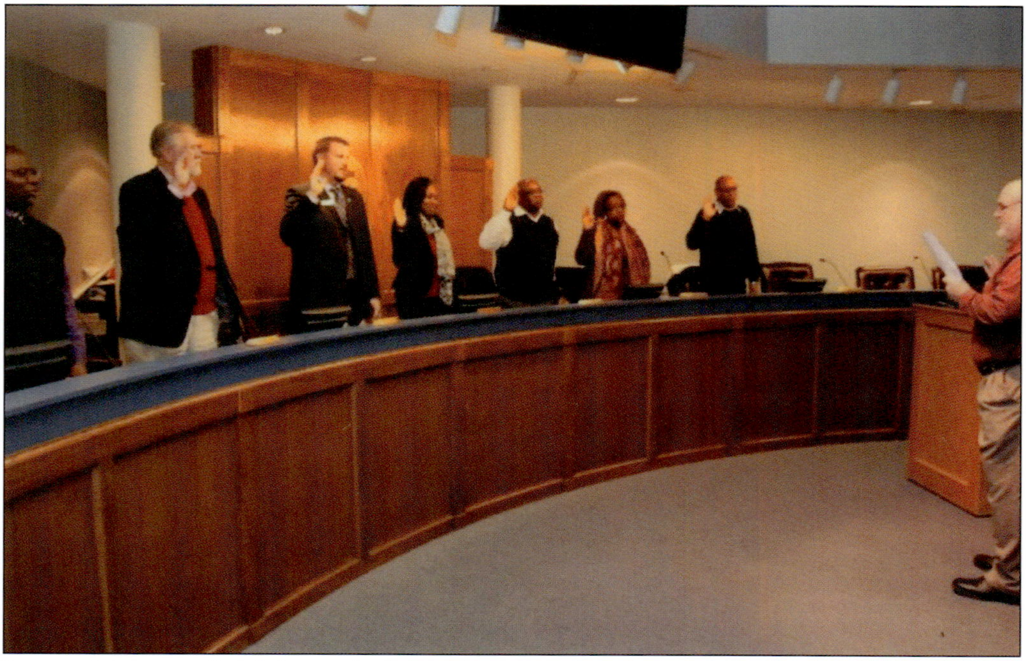

Justice of the peace Bob Johnson (right) swears in members of the new Jacksonville-North Pulaski School Board at Jacksonville City Hall in 2014. From left to right are Richard Moss, Dr. Robert Price, Daniel Gray (president), LaConda Watson, Norris Cain, Carol Miles, and Ron McDaniel (vice president). (Courtesy of the *Leader*.)

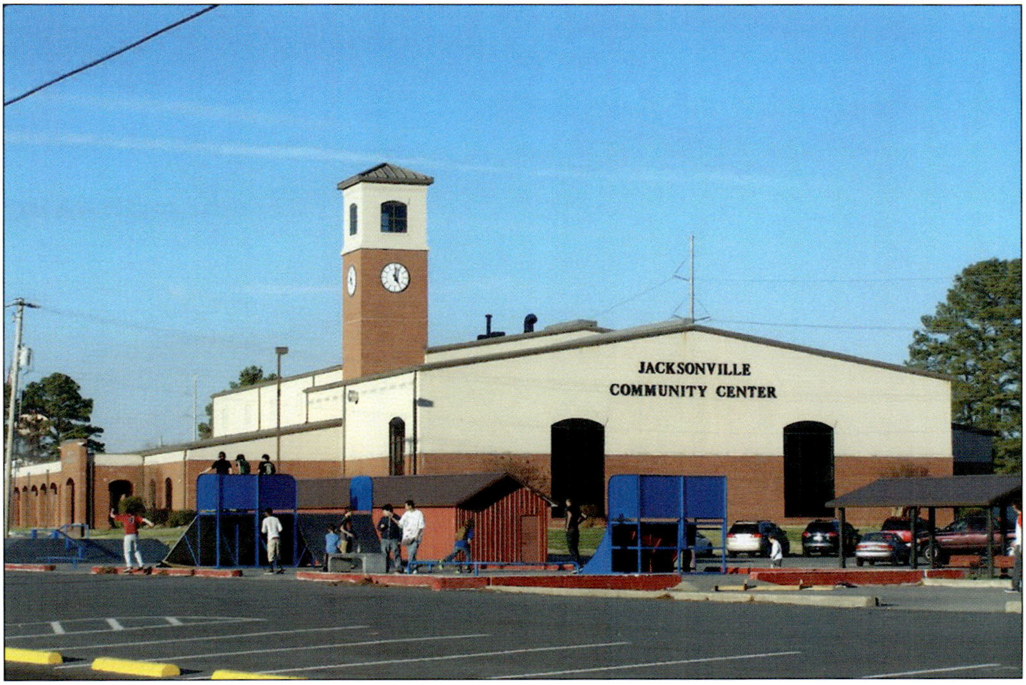

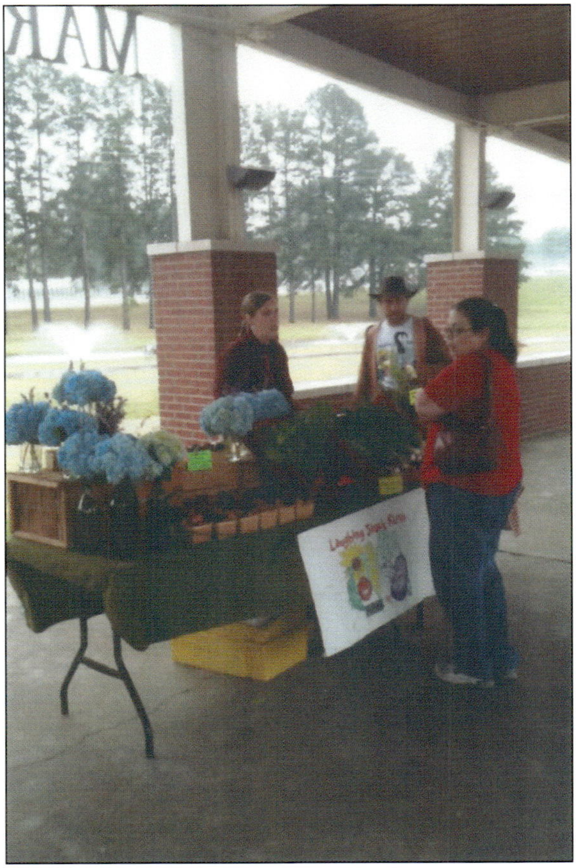

Above, the skate park, built in 2005, is located beside the Jacksonville Community Center and is used by kids of all ages for the purpose of skateboarding. At right is the Jacksonville Farmers' Market, which was built in 2010 for local vendors to sell produce and goods. One of the farms active at the market is Laughing Stock Farms. (Courtesy of the Jacksonville Parks and Recreation Department.)

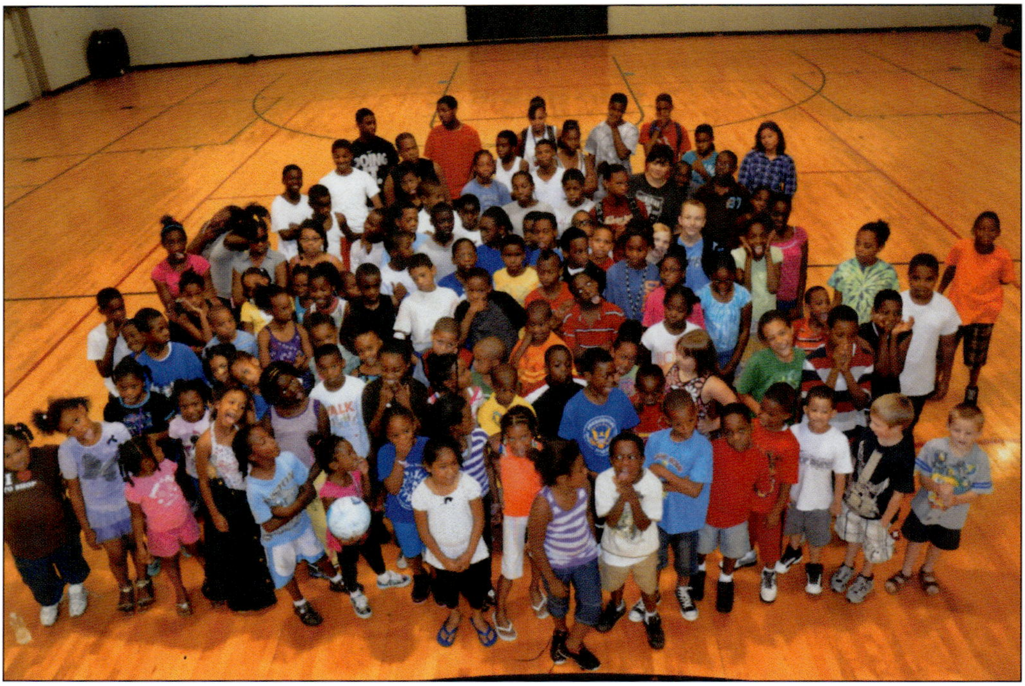

The Boys and Girls Club of Jacksonville is a positive place for children. The club provides both a summer and after-school program, as well as a youth basketball program. (Courtesy of the Jacksonville Boys and Girls Club.)

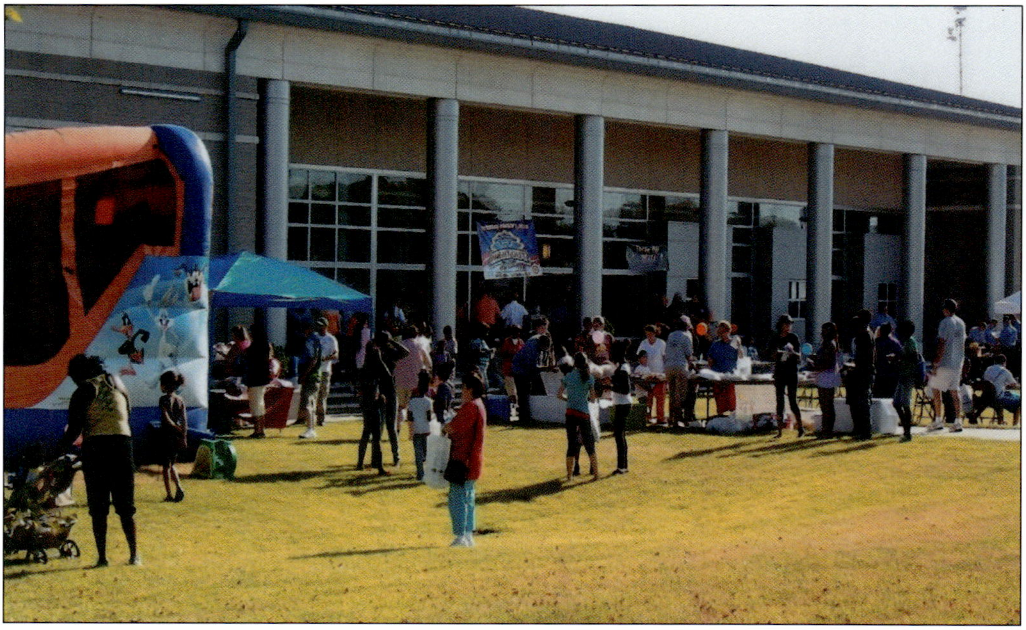

National Night Out 2011, held at the Esther D. Nixon Library, was sponsored by Westside Baptist Church, Evangelistic Church, the Methodist church, Jacksonville Police and Fire Departments, the library, and Warren Street Neighbors. It is all about safety for children and adults who call Jacksonville home. There are about 400 people that show up yearly. (Courtesy of Warren Street Neighbors.)

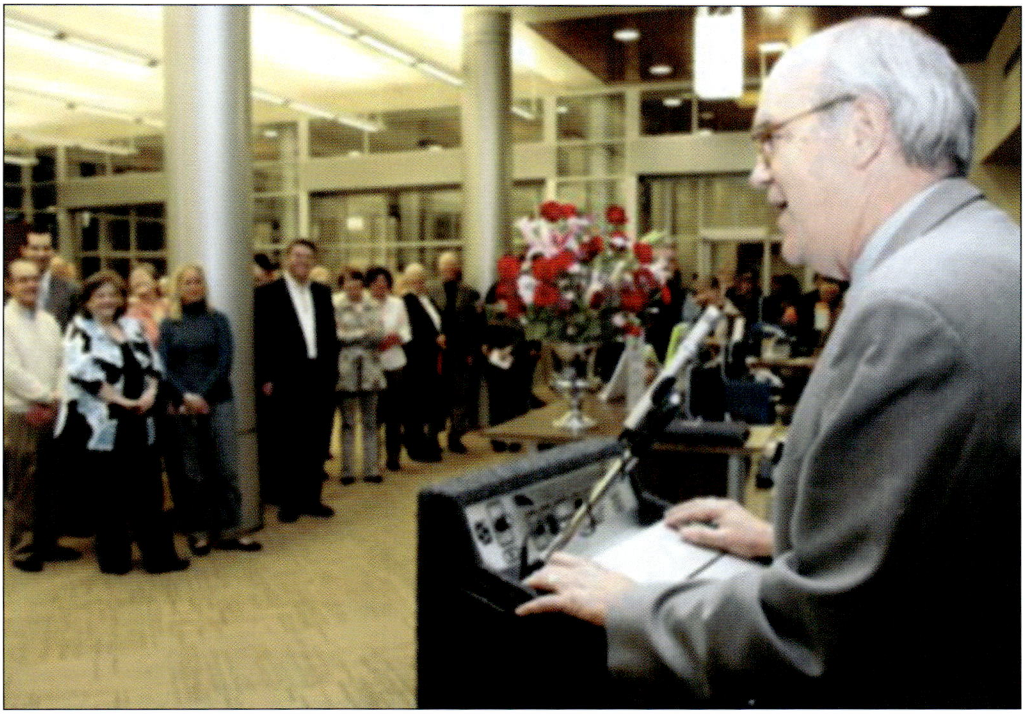

Above, Bobby Roberts, director of the Central Arkansas Library System, addresses a group gathered for a reception in February marking the grand opening of the new Esther D. Nixon Library, located at 703 West Main Street. Below is an exterior view of the new facility. (Courtesy of the Esther D. Nixon Library.)

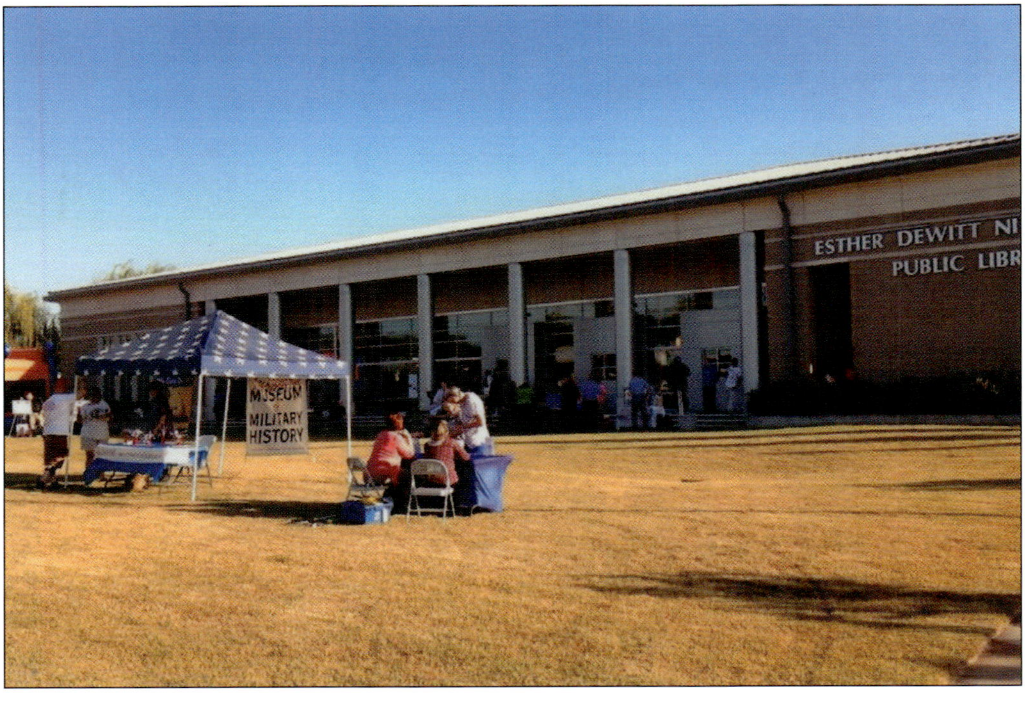

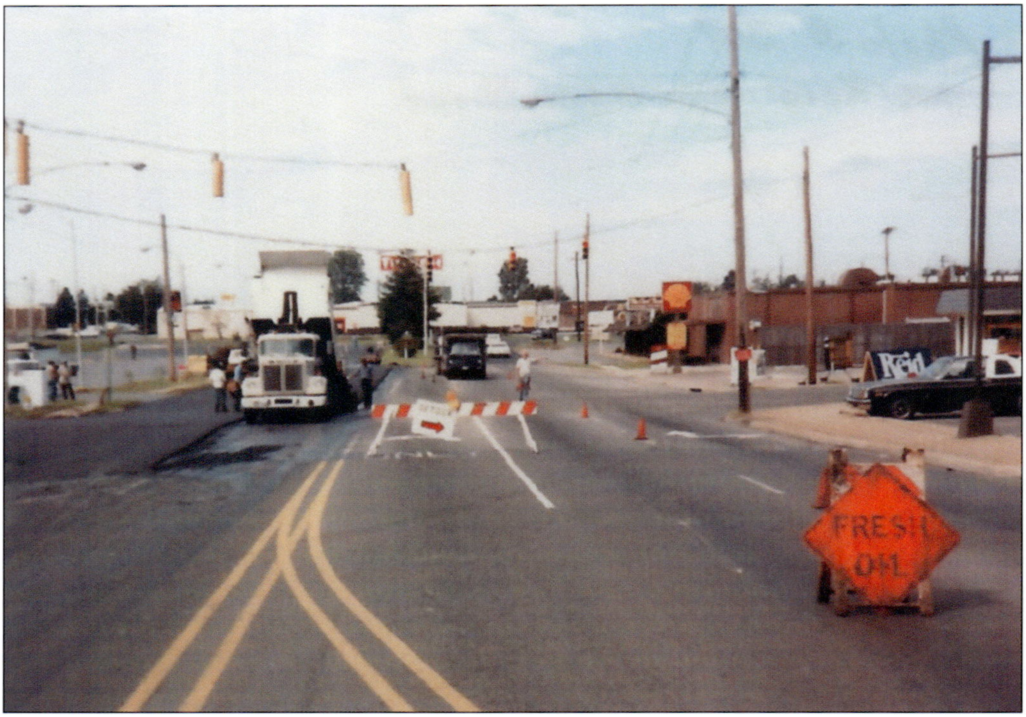

Street workers are pictured here on Main Street with Firestone auto care in the background, which was built on the front part of the Arkansas Ordnance Plant land. This image provides an idea of what the main intersection in town looked like in the 1970s. (Courtesy of the Jacksonville Public Works Department.)

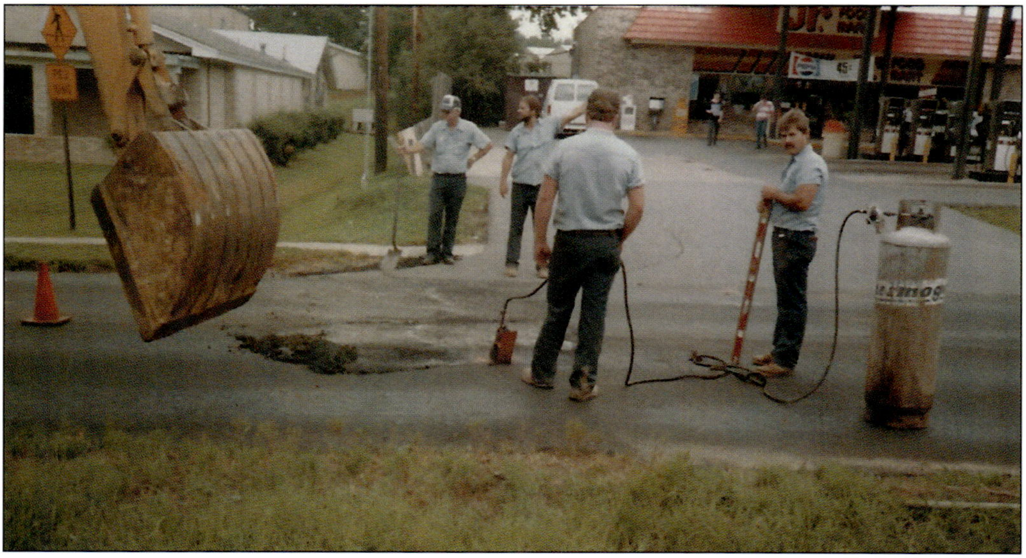

The Jacksonville Public Works fixes drainage issues in town, which is critical during heavy rains so that there is no flooding. Maintaining the roadways has always been a priority of city officials. (Courtesy of the Jacksonville Public Works Department.)

Four

MILITARY

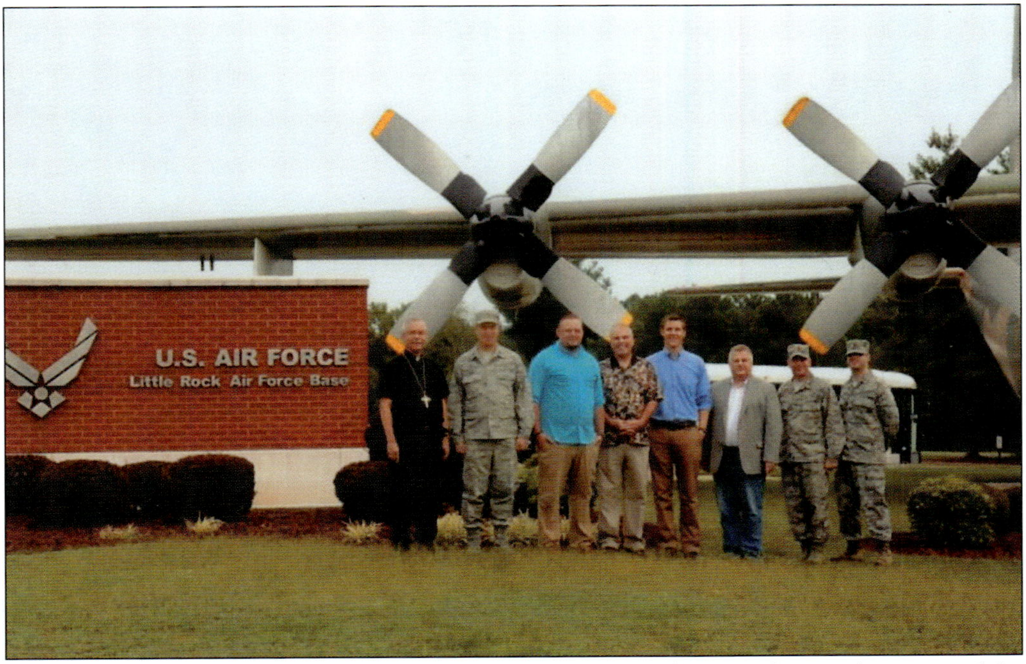

Little Rock Air Force Base opened on October 9, 1955. Pictured here at the new front gate of the base are pastors from area churches, who are taking a tour of the base in early 2000. (Courtesy of Little Rock Air Force Base.)

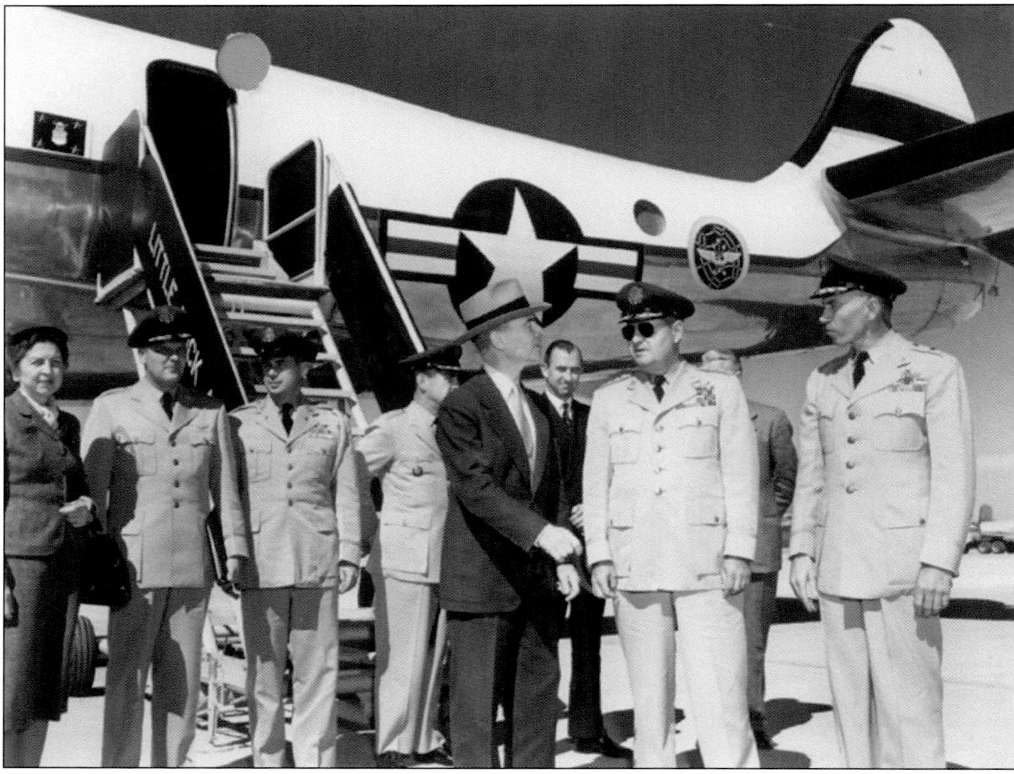

Pictured here is opening day of Little Rock Air Force Base on October 9, 1955, with many dignitaries in attendance. (Courtesy of Little Rock Air Force Base.)

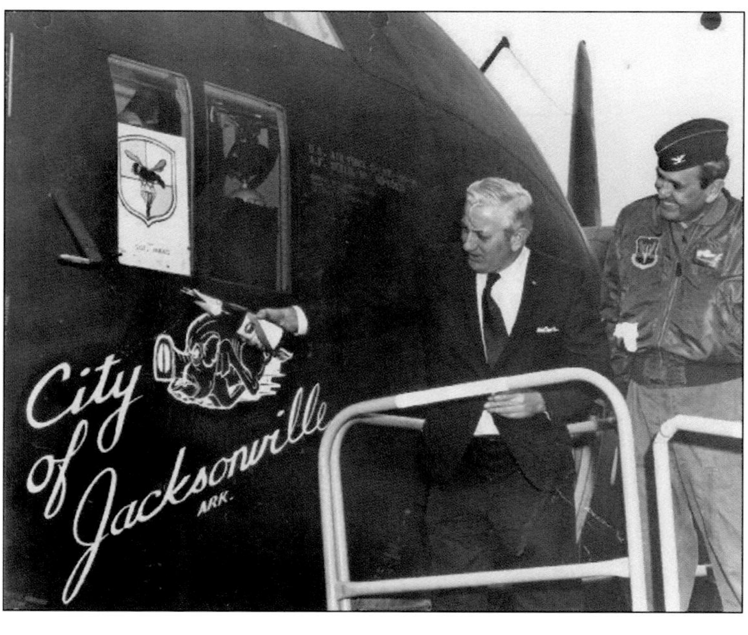

In 1970, Mayor John Hardin christens the first 64th Tactical Airlift Wing C-130 Hercules to arrive at Little Rock Air Force Base as the *City of Jacksonville*, while Col. Richard J. Gibney, commander of the 64th, looks on. This marked the beginning of the C-130 era at the base in Jacksonville, Arkansas. (Courtesy of Little Rock Air Force Base.)

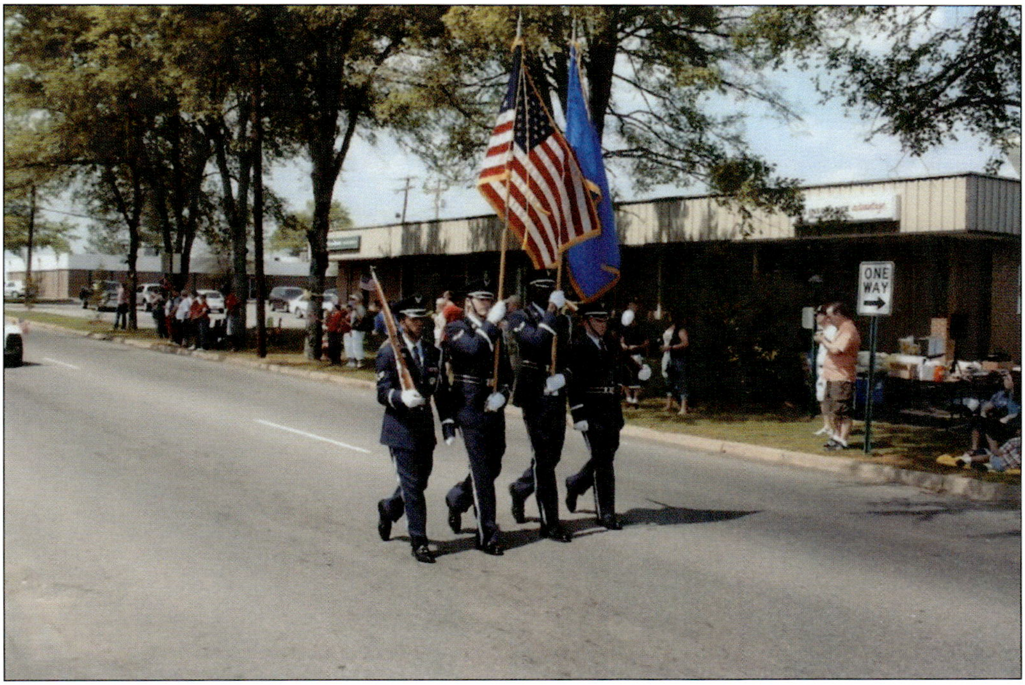

Veterans participate in the Welcome Home Vietnam Veterans parade. The event honored the more than three million Americans who served during the Vietnam War. Attendees paid tribute to those who were laid to rest and showed a generation of veterans the respect and support of a grateful nation. (Courtesy of A1c. Cliffton Dolezal.)

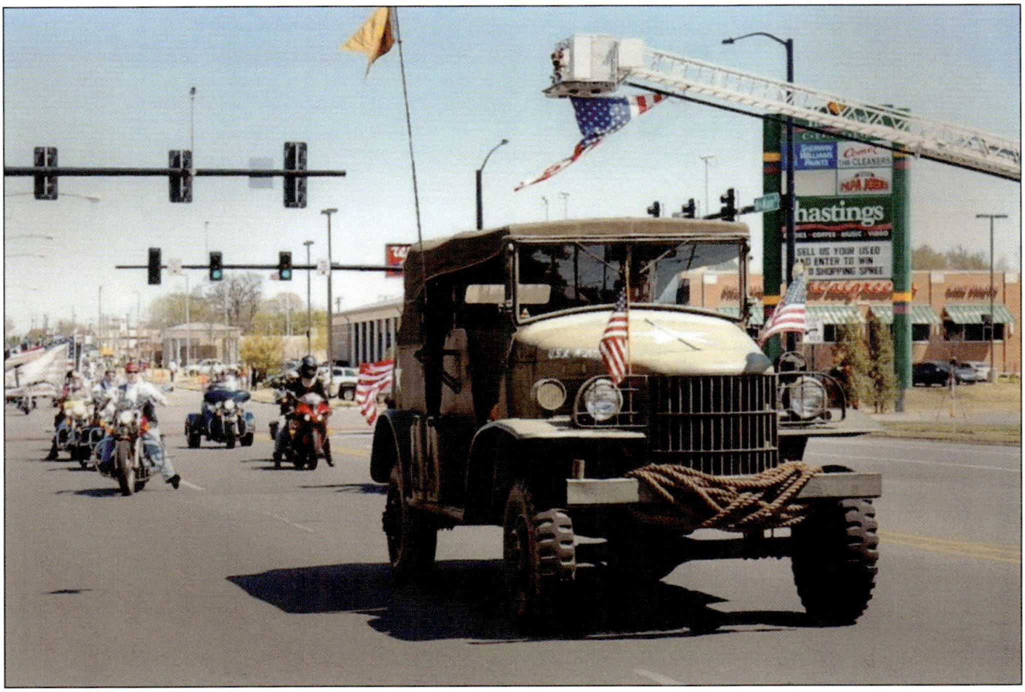

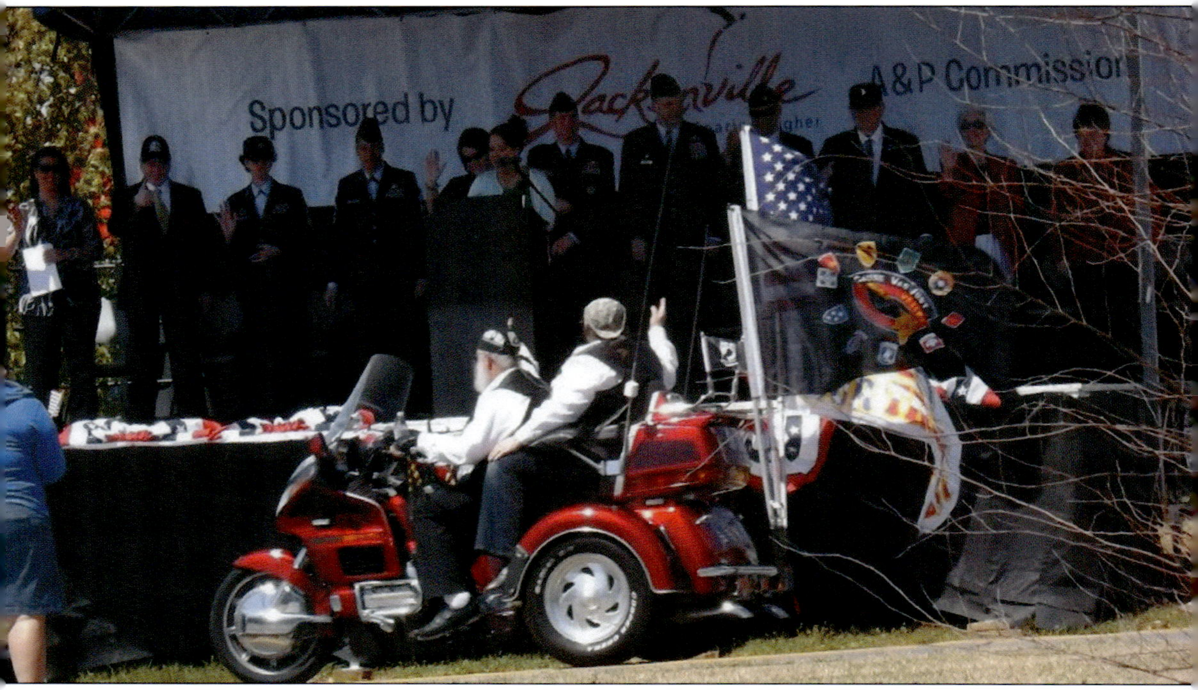

The parade, which lasted about 30 minutes, had about 20 groups take part, including the Little Rock Air Force Base Honor Guard; parade marshal John Mohler, who earned three Purple Hearts during multiple tours in Vietnam; the Rolling Thunder and Combat Veterans motorcycle club; the David D. Terry Jr. chapter of the Air Force Association, which sponsored a decorated truck; and a truck and trailer by A Veteran's Best Friend, a nonprofit dedicated to using service dogs to help Vietnam veterans lead normal lives. (Courtesy of Rick Kron.)

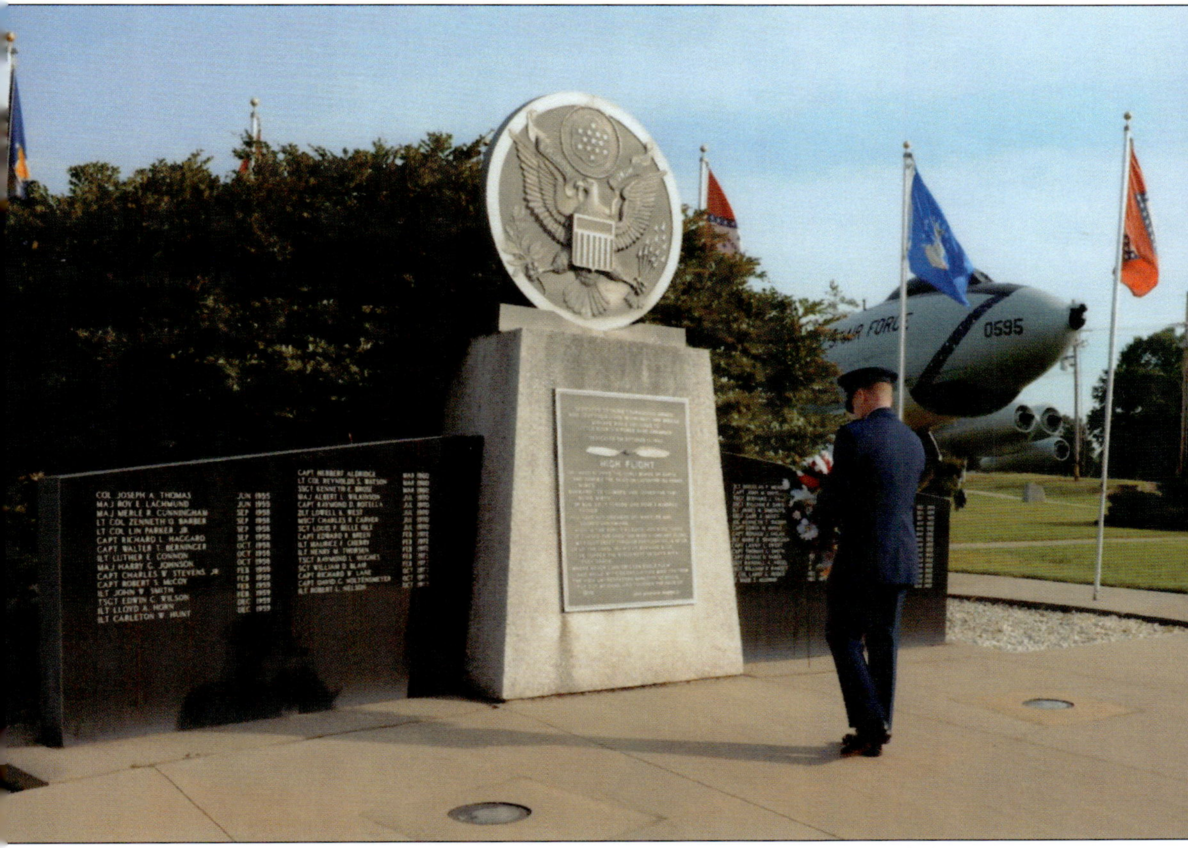

In observance of Memorial Day, Team Little Rock honored the fallen at a wreath-laying ceremony at three different memorials in Heritage Park. In this photograph, Col. Patrick Rhatigan, the 19th Airlift Wing commander, carries a wreath during the ceremony. (Courtesy of Little Rock Air Force Base.)

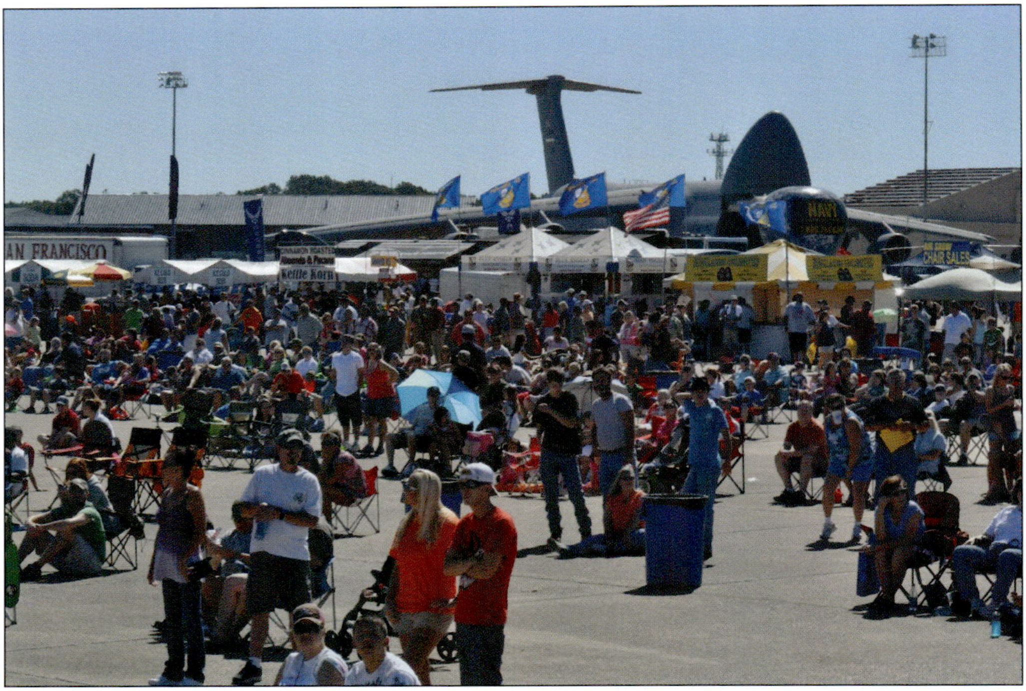

A crowd watches the Heritage and Heroes Open House and Air Show at Little Rock Air Force Base as the Blue Angels give a spectacular performance. The air show, one of the largest public events in Arkansas, was estimated to have attracted more than 200,000 attendees throughout the weekend each year. Unfortunately, as of a few years ago, the base no longer puts on the air show. (Courtesy of S.Sgt. Jacob Barreiro and S.Sgt. Jessica Condit.)

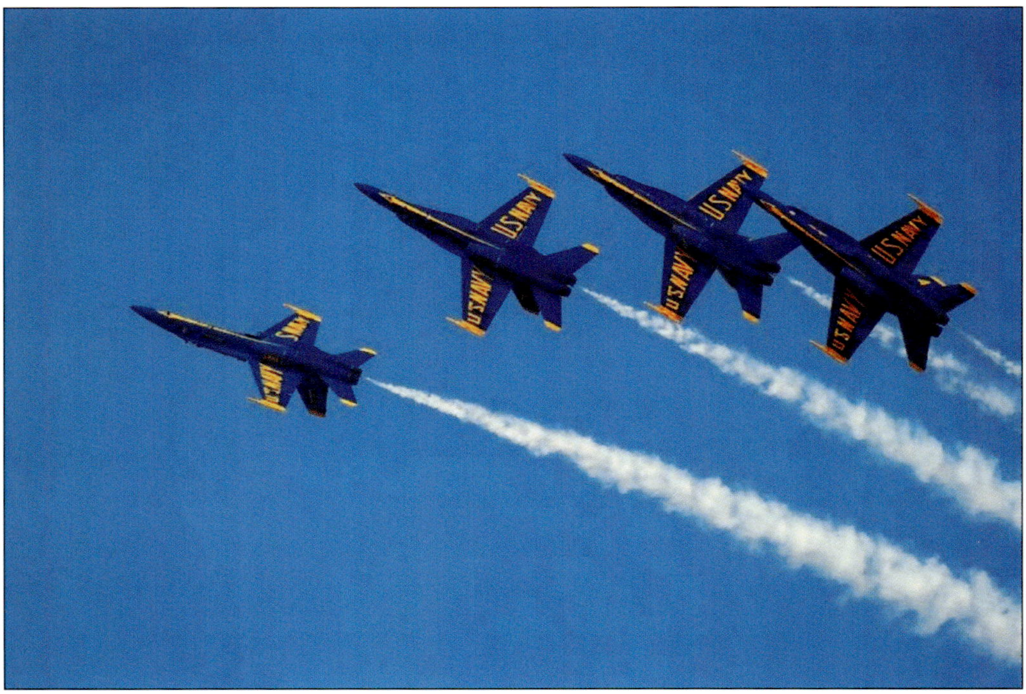

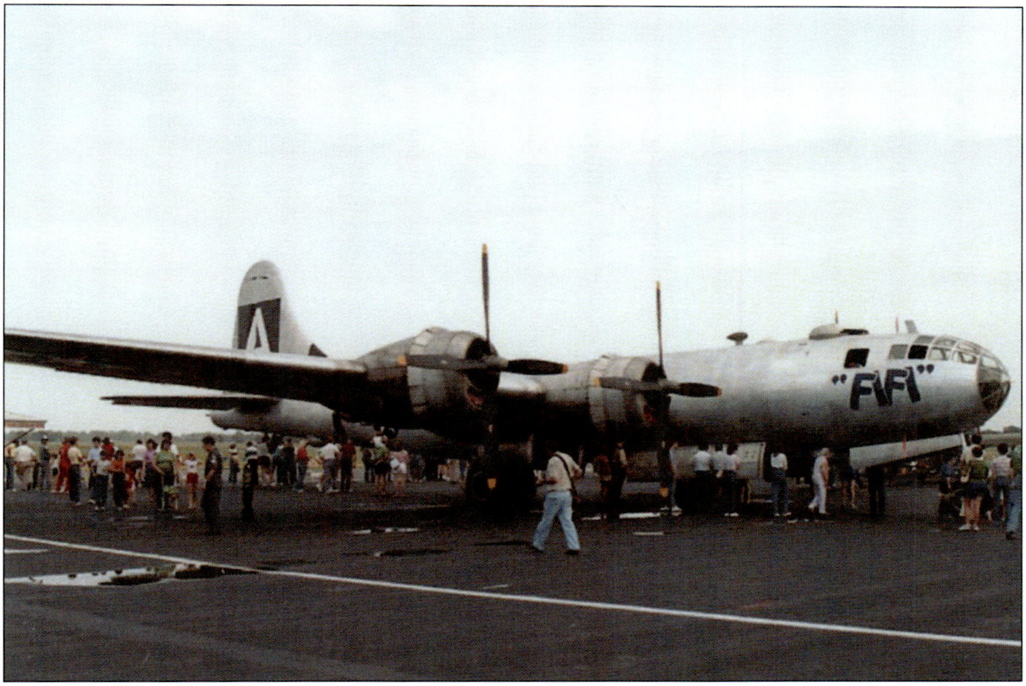

A Boeing B-29 Super-fortress named *FI-FI* is pictured here at an air show at Little Rock Air Force Base in 1985, giving people the chance to see the magnificent aircraft. (Courtesy of Ed Uthman.)

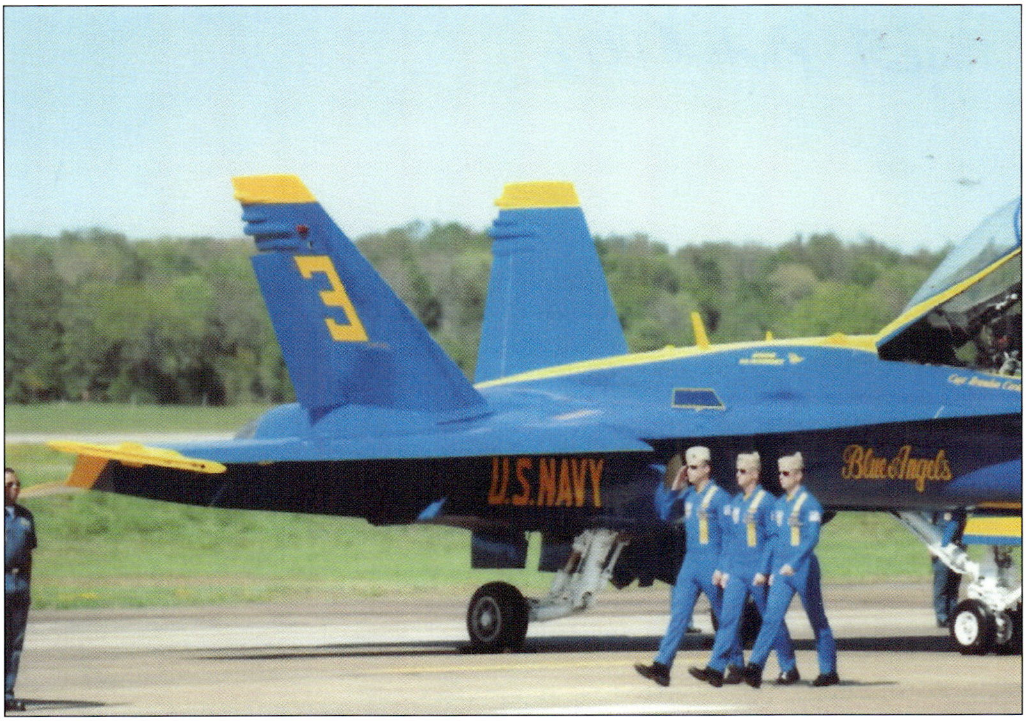

US Navy Blue Angel pilots walk to their aircraft. They performed during the Heritage and Heroes Open House and Air Show in 1985. (Courtesy of Ed Uthman.)

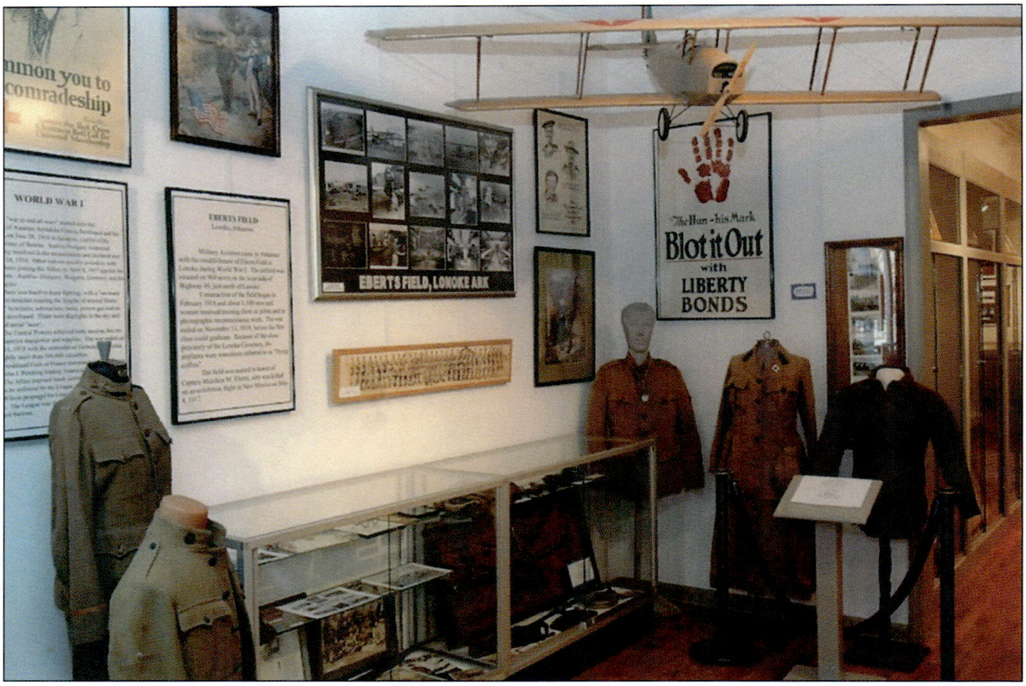

The Jacksonville Museum of Military History gallery is pictured here. In addition to the museum, there is a store, media presentation and projection room, and a research library. (Courtesy of the Jacksonville Museum of Military History.)

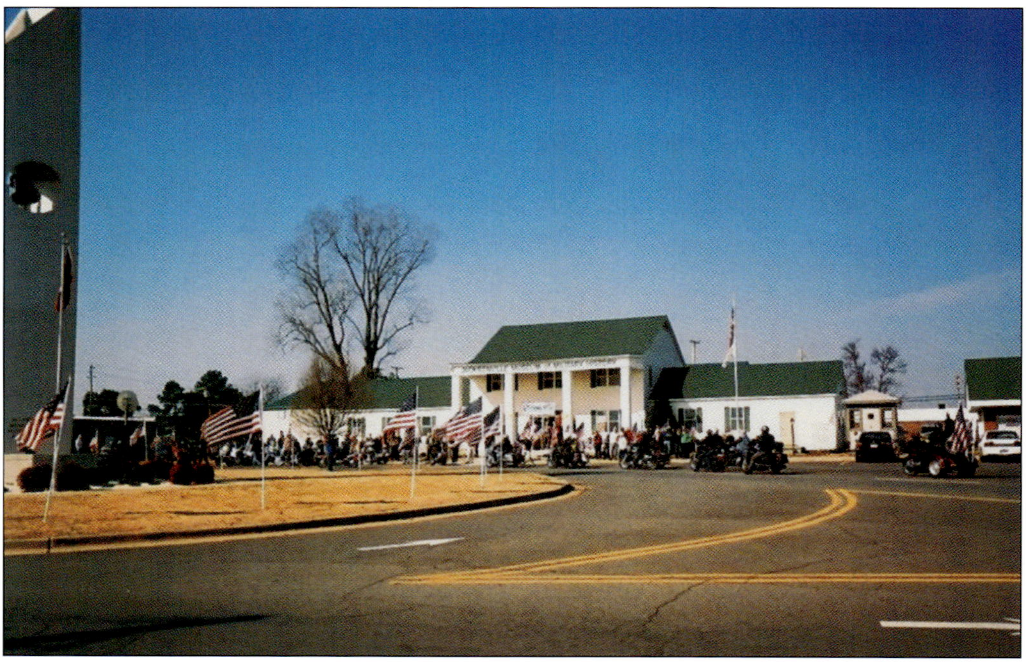

The museum, which opened in May 2005, is located on the site of the administration building of the Jacksonville Ordnance Plant in World War II. The motorcycle riders seen here are in front of the building before the start of the veterans parade. (Courtesy of the Jacksonville Museum of Military History.)

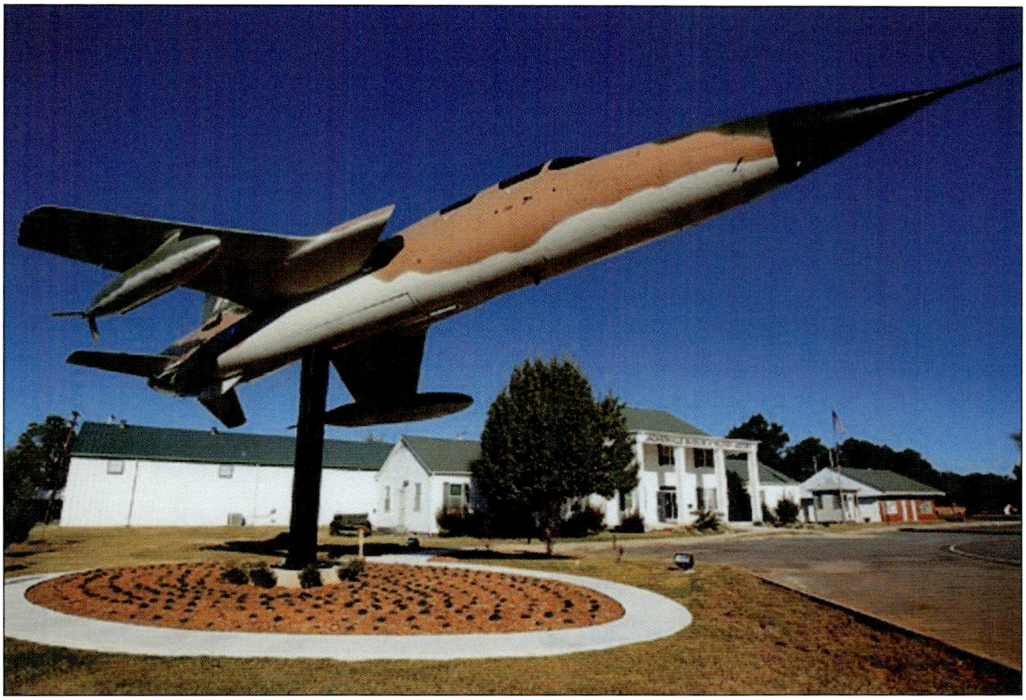

This is an F-105 Thunderchief donated to the museum by Little Rock Air Force Base in a ceremony with Col. Leo Thorsness (retired), who was a prisoner of war for six years during World War II. (Courtesy of the Jacksonville Museum of Military History.)

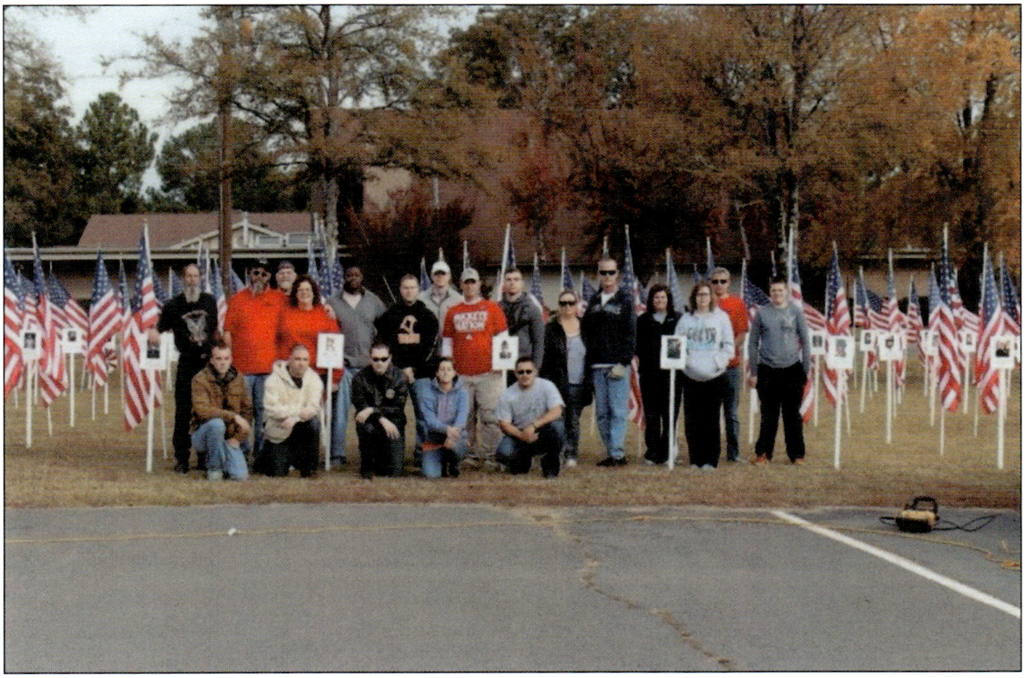

Pictured here is the team that helped set up the memorial at the Jacksonville Museum of Military History. The care and commitment each of them has for honoring fallen heroes is beyond words. (Courtesy of the Jacksonville Museum of Military History.)

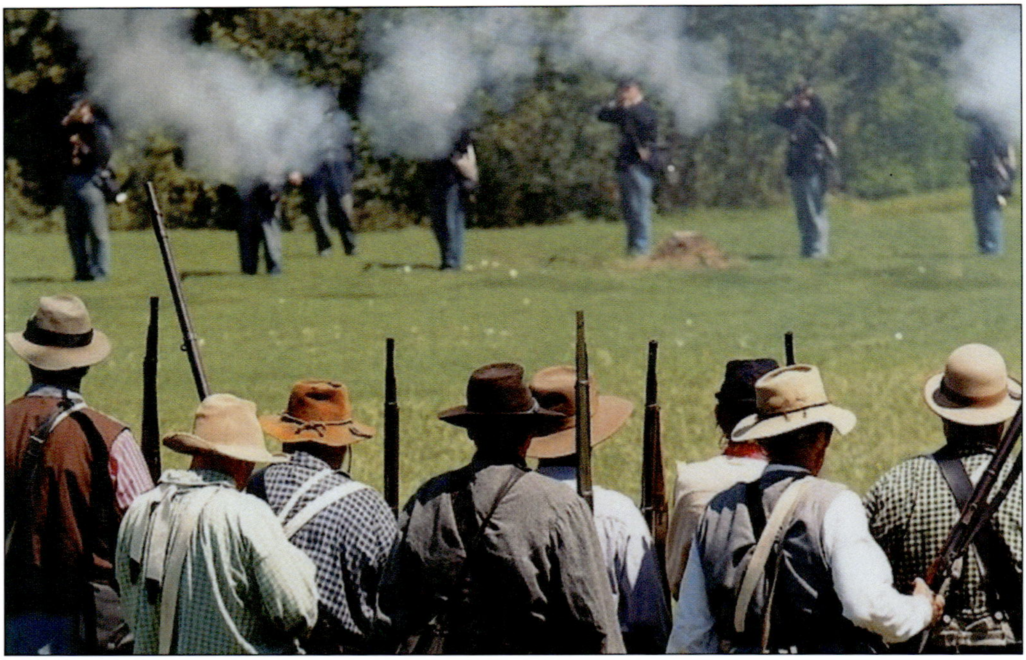

Pictured here in 1970 is a reenactment of the battle took place on Bayou Meto, on the south side of Jacksonville, at Reed's Bridge in August 1863. The Confederates, led by Brig. Gen. John S. Marmaduke, held back Union troops, forcing them to find a new route to Little Rock. Reed's Bridge was torched, and at least nine men lost their lives during the battle. The town has reenactment battles every year at this time. (Courtesy of Susan Davitt.)

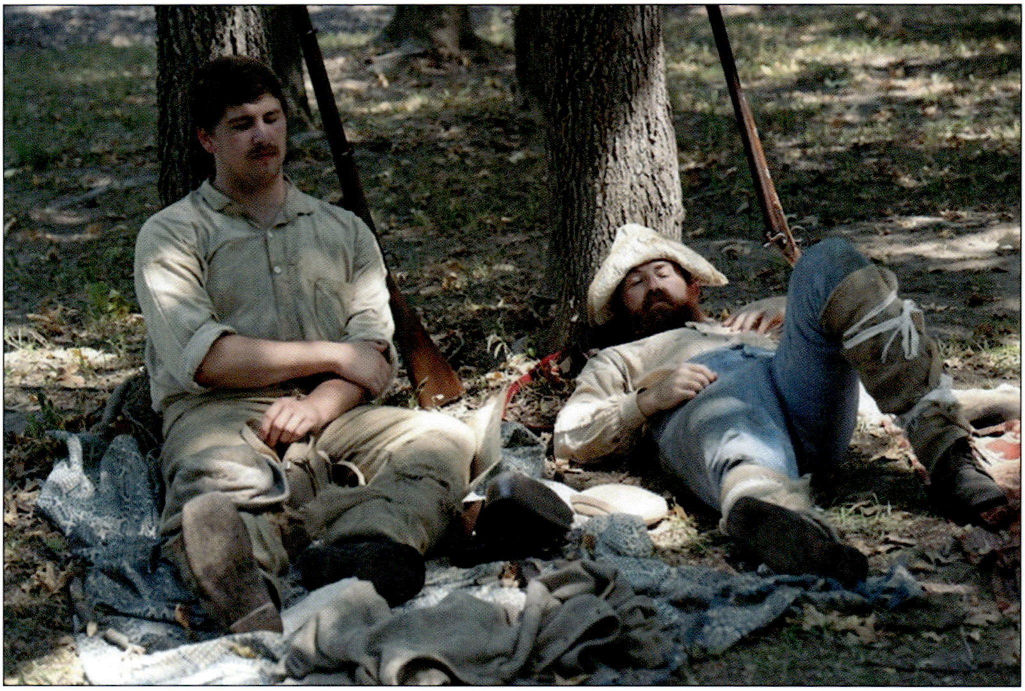

Wounded men are pictured at the reenactment of the battle took place on Bayou Meto. (Courtesy of Reed's Bridge Battlefield Heritage Park.)

Five

Service Industry

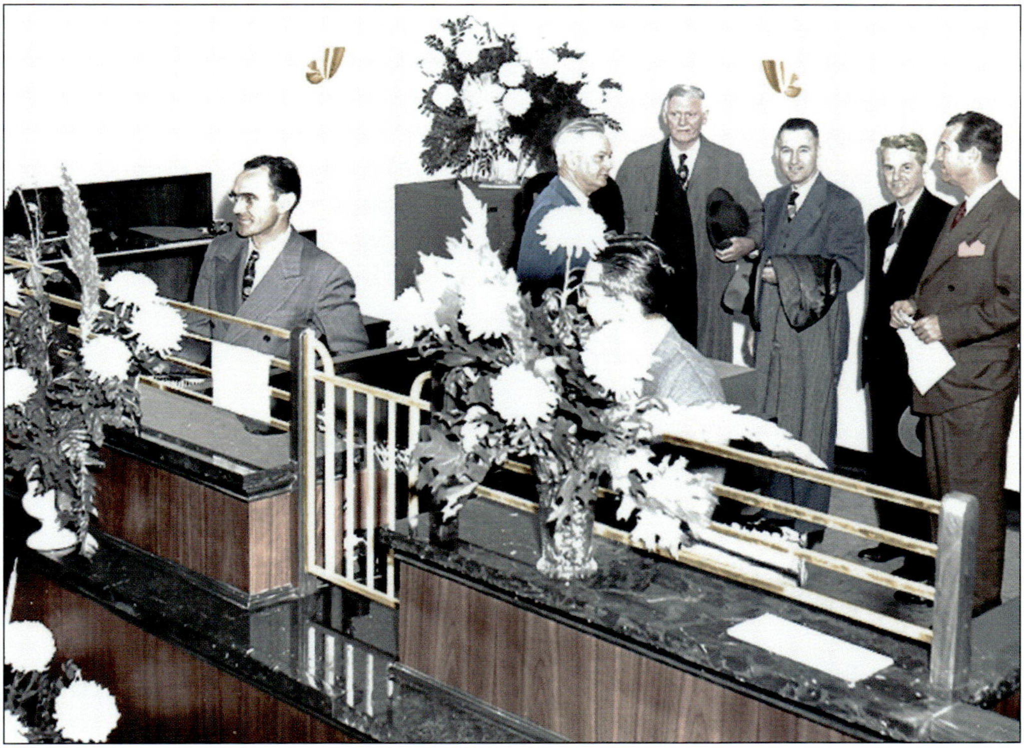

On November 5, 1949, the first Jacksonville State Bank opened in a new building on the south side of Main Street, a half block west of First Street. Bankers from other towns, officials of the state bank department, and local dignitaries attended the opening ceremonies. Many of the community's residents were thrilled to have a local bank at last, and numerous persons opened checking accounts there on the first day. The man in the brown suit is Raymond Rebsamen. (Courtesy of First Arkansas Bank and Trust.)

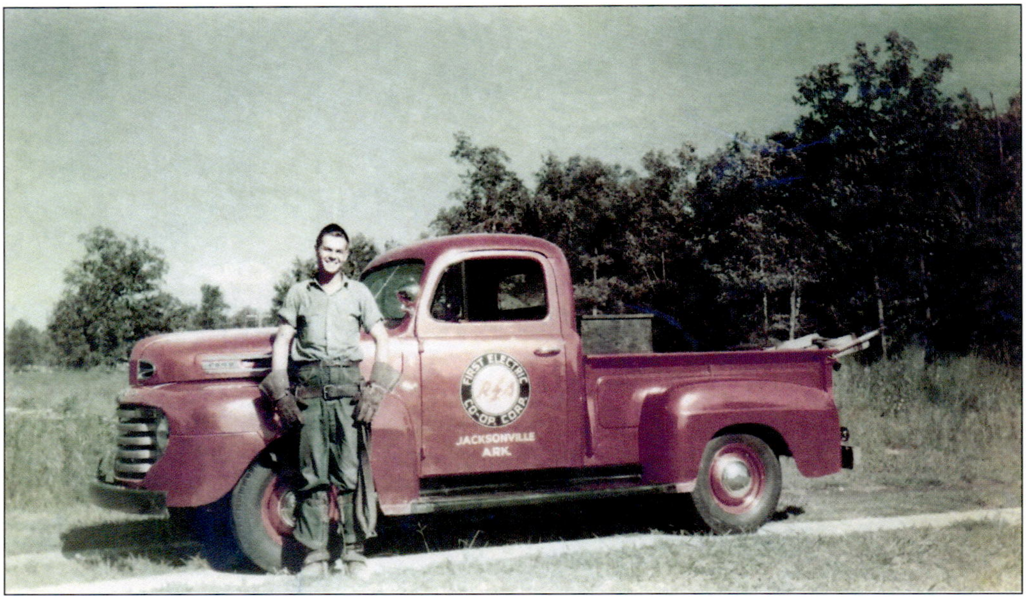

Above, lineman Bill Brown displays a new truck in 1948. Below are First Electric employees in 1970, including Bobby Taylor, Joe Leman, Robert Love, Roger Skiver, Lloyd Jones, Robert Cole, Jim Bennett, and W.A. Brown. Today, First Electric's fleet includes 52 bucket trucks and 16 digger derricks. (Courtesy of First Electric.)

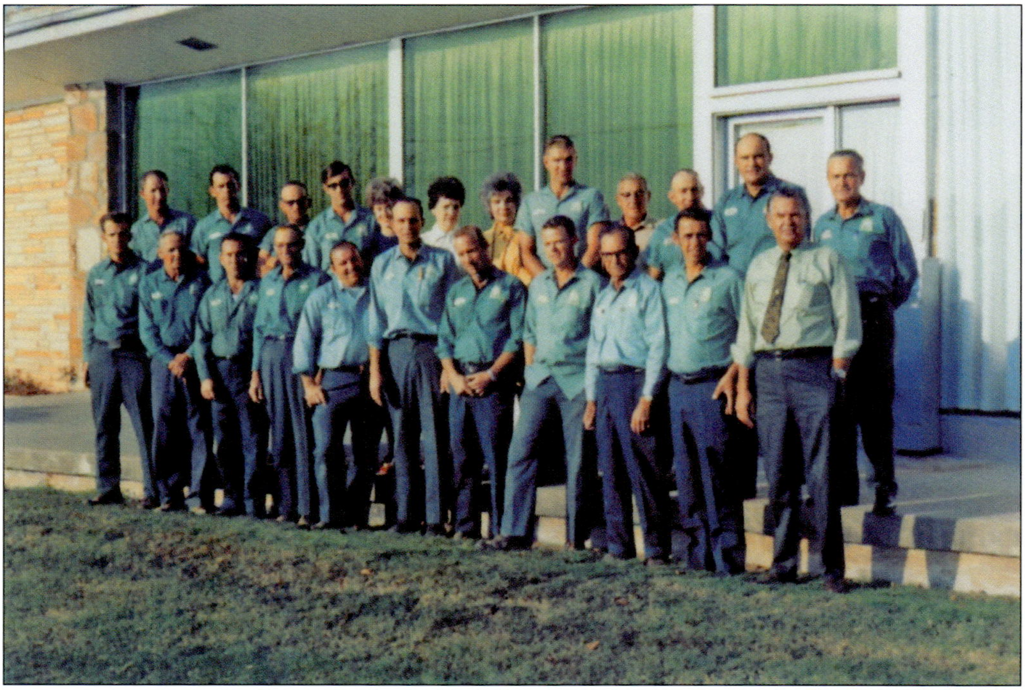

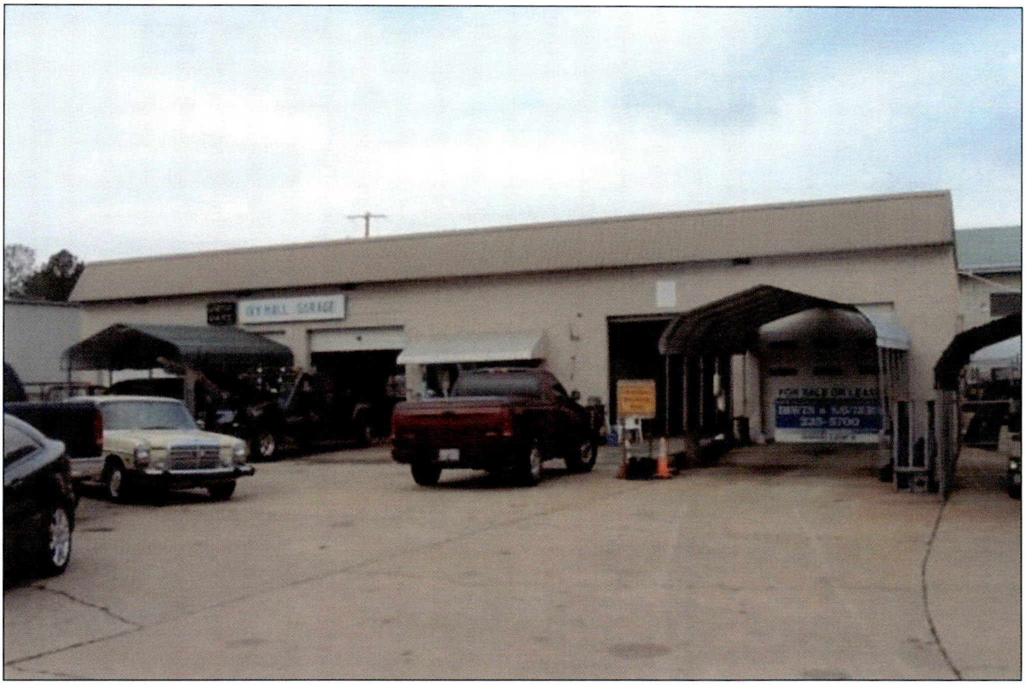

Ivy Halls Wrecker Service is a family-owned business, located at 1100 West Main Street, with William Hall as the current president. The business also performs auto care. (Courtesy of the Jacksonville Historical District.)

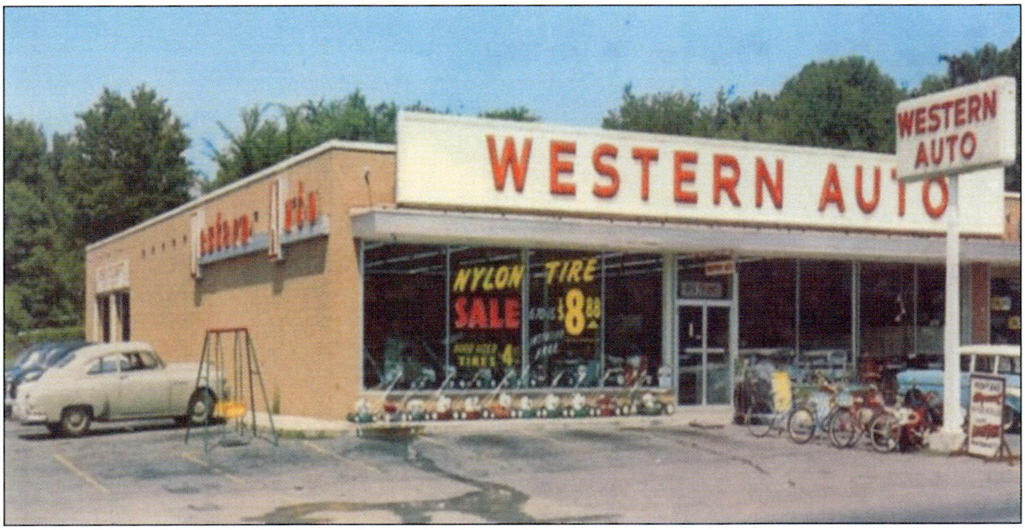

Western Auto Store, owned by Harry Daughtery, started out at 104 South First Street before moving in the 1960s to the corner of Main and Warren Streets across from First Arkansas Bank and Trust. (Courtesy of the Jacksonville Historical District.)

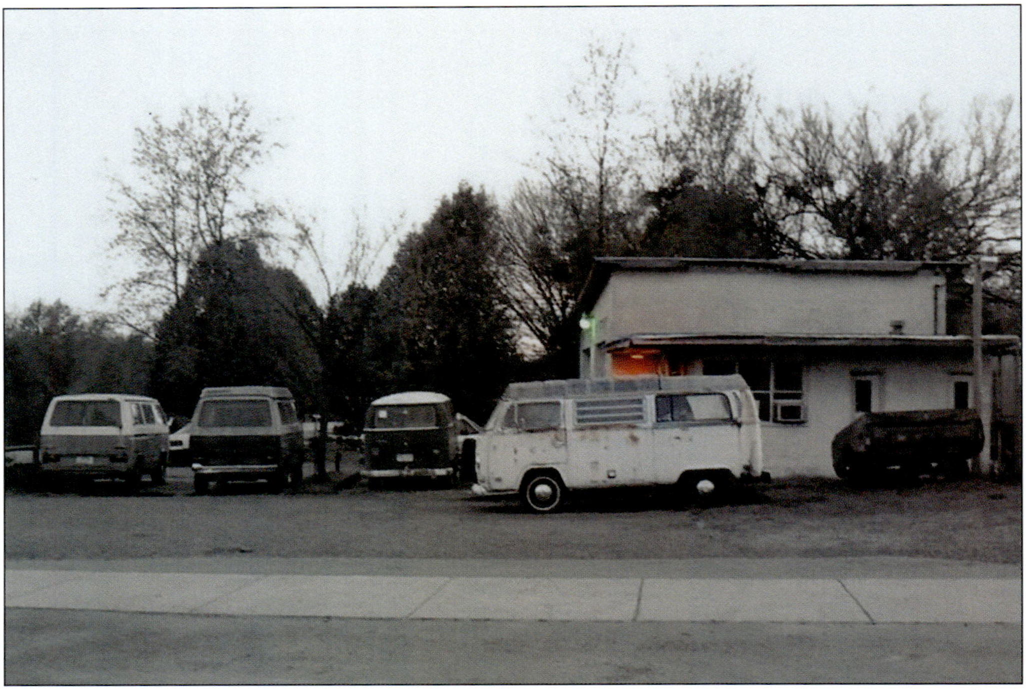

A family-owned business started in 1977, Adams Foreign Car Repair's first owner was William Adams. After his death, Johnny James bought the First Street business from Mrs. Adams, and it is still owned by him today. (Courtesy of the Jacksonville Historical District.)

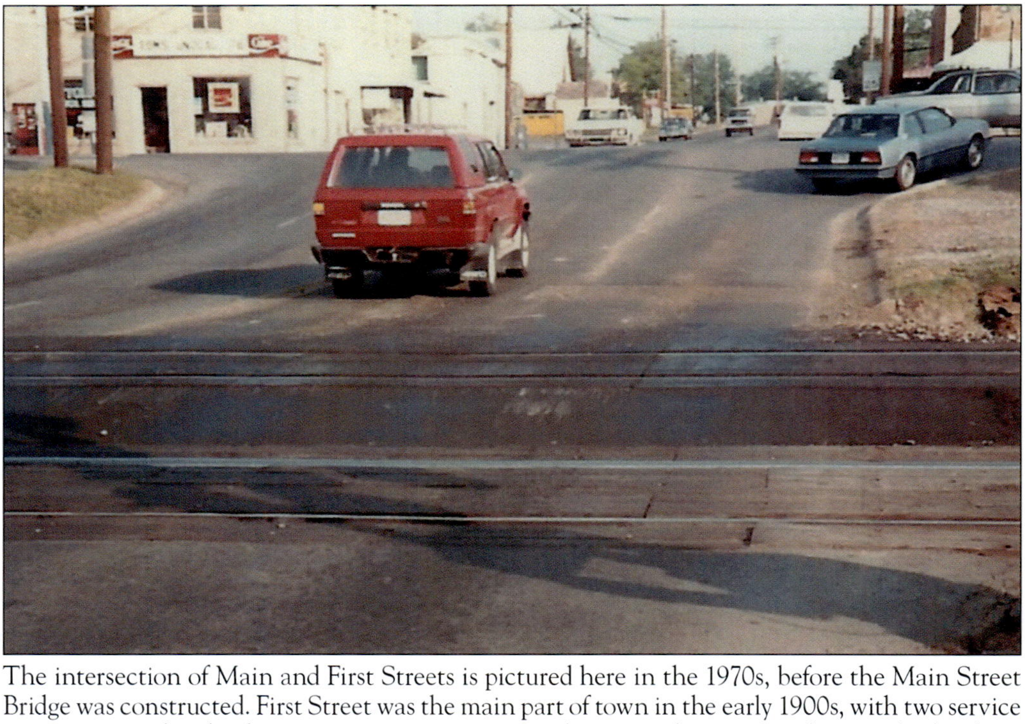

The intersection of Main and First Streets is pictured here in the 1970s, before the Main Street Bridge was constructed. First Street was the main part of town in the early 1900s, with two service stations on each side, department stores, grocery and mercantile stores, and even a barbershop. (Courtesy of Jacksonville Engineering.)

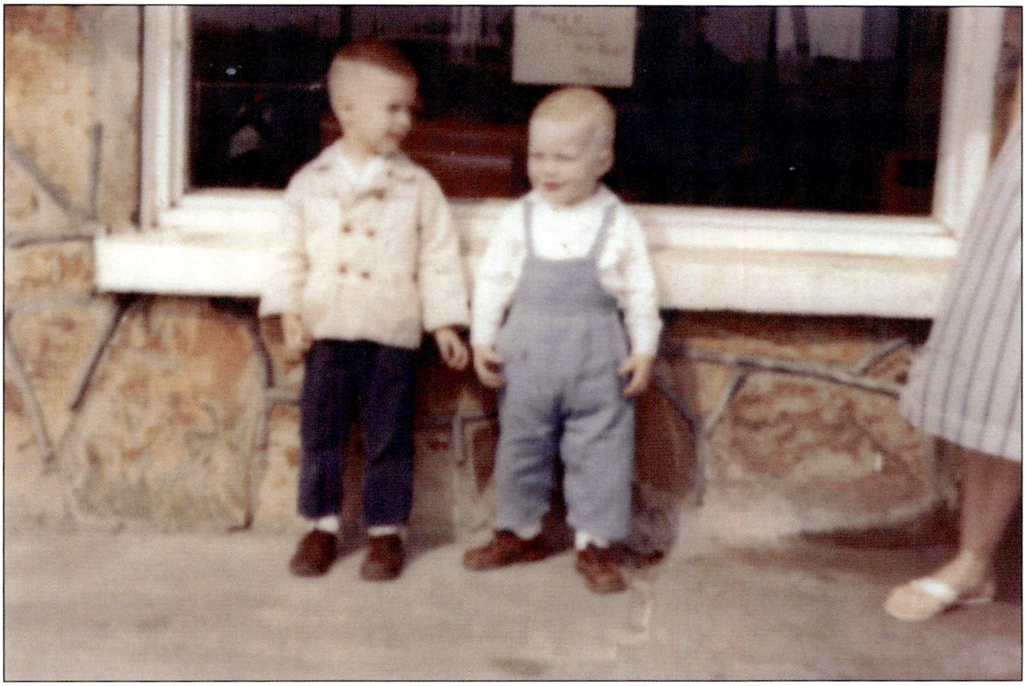

Jim (left) and Jerry Hansen are pictured here in front of the rock garage on First Street, the sons of a former owner of the Hansen Mobil service station. (Courtesy of Jim Hansen.)

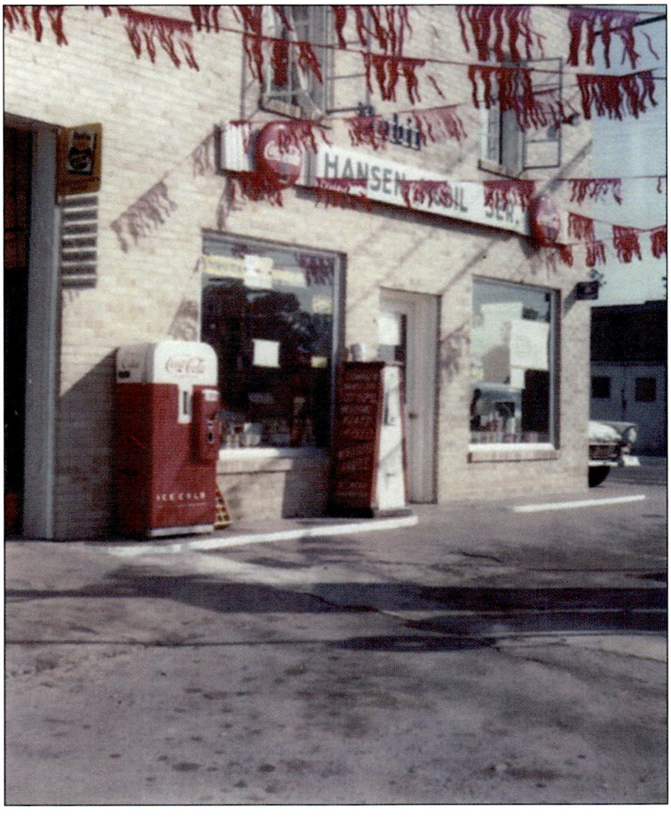

Pictured here in the 1960s, Hansen service station was a daily stop for some children on their way to school before it was torn down to make way for the Main Street Bridge. Over the years, it has had several owners, including Bennett Douglas, Jim Hansen, Harold Means, and Tommy Waller. (Courtesy of Jim Hansen.)

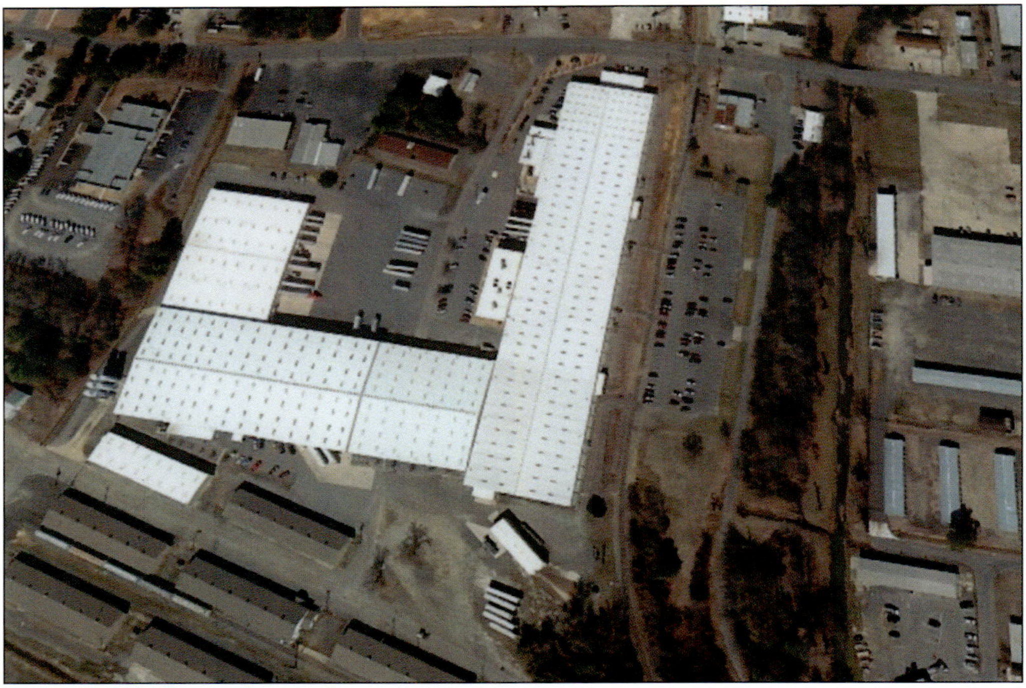

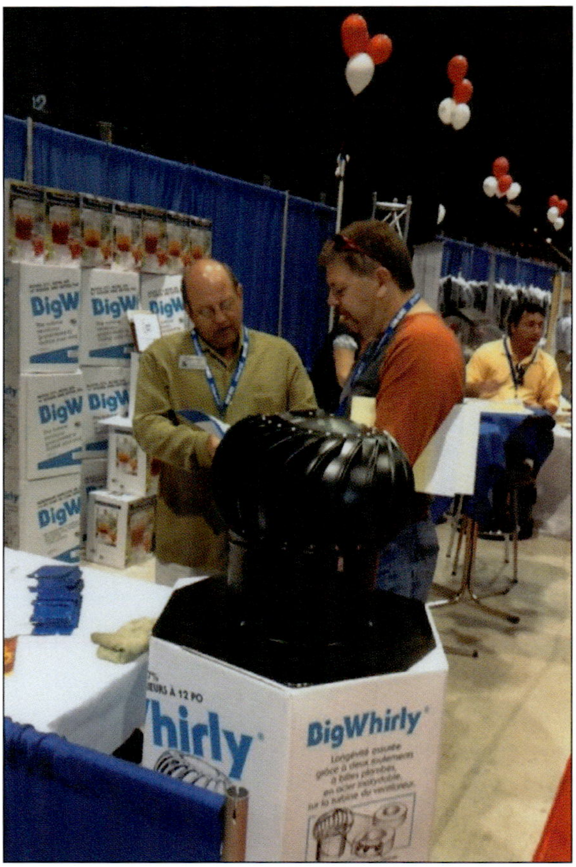

Above is an aerial view of the Lomanco plant. Lomanco, which opened in Jacksonville in 1966, makes industrial and commercial fans, blowers, and air-purification equipment. Owner Ted Belden, who started the business in his garage, is pictured at left (on the left) at the Can Save 2012 Expo. (Courtesy of Mike Traylor.)

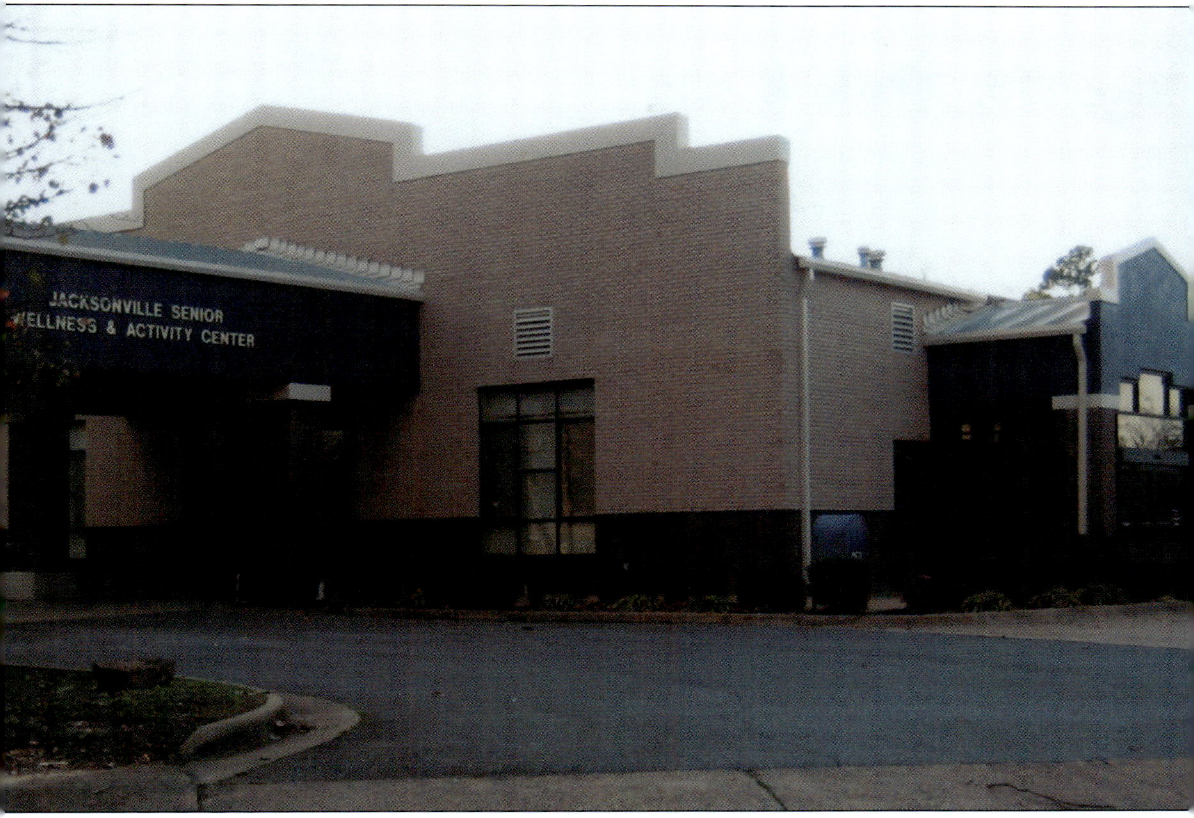

Jacksonville Senior Wellness Activity Center is located where the Graco Theater was located before it burned in 1980. The property at 109 Victory Circle was occupied just four years later by the senior center. In 2013, a tornado shelter safe room was added for area residents the tenants of the senior center. (Courtesy of the Jacksonville Historical District.)

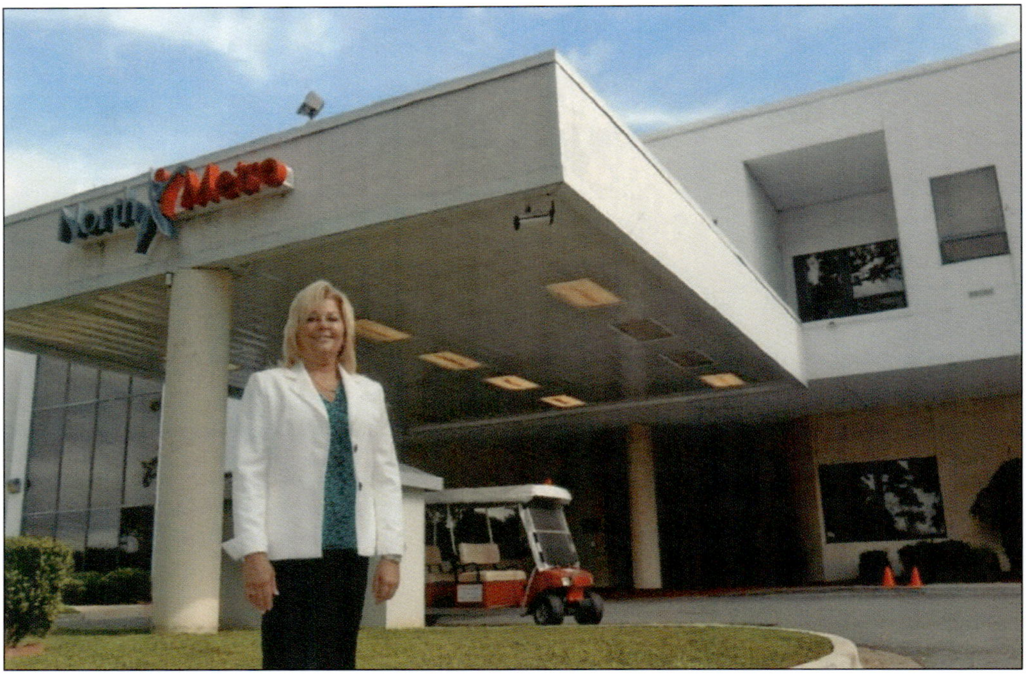

Cindy Stafford, pictured above in front of the hospital she has worked at for 14 years, was hired as North Metro Medical Center's chief executive officer in April 1999. The hospital has grown since it first opened its doors on January 24, 1962, as Rebsamen Memorial Hospital. It originally had 30 beds and 17 employees. The land was donated by Raymond Rebsamen, and a local bond issue was approved by city voters. Today, the hospital is a 113-bed acute-care facility with over 500 employees and 200 physicians on staff. Below is a view of the lobby. (Courtesy of North Metro Hospital.)

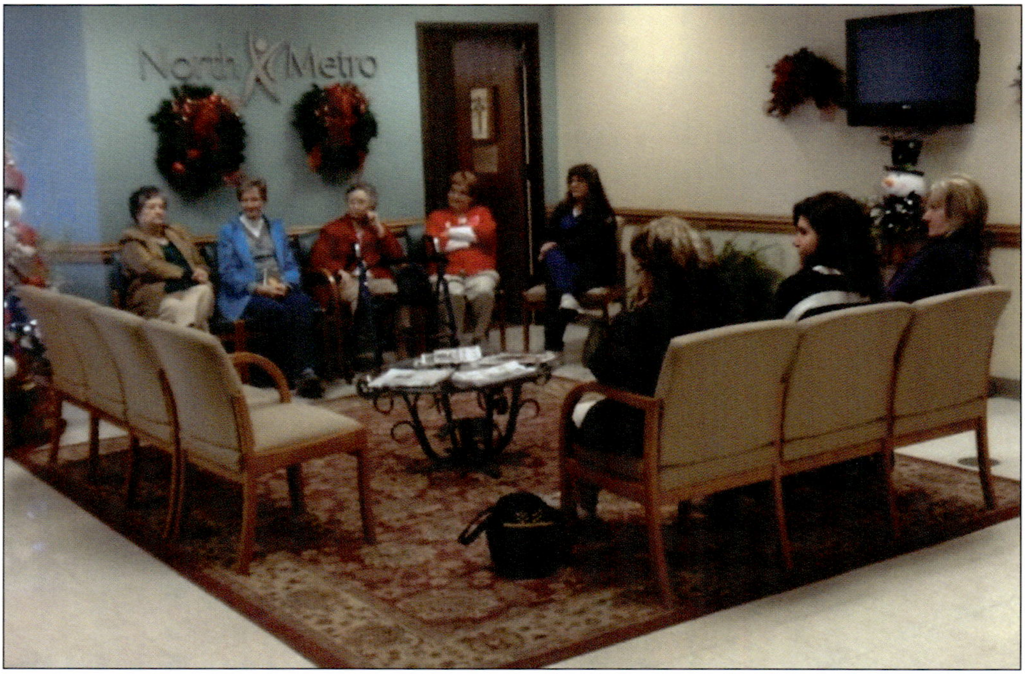

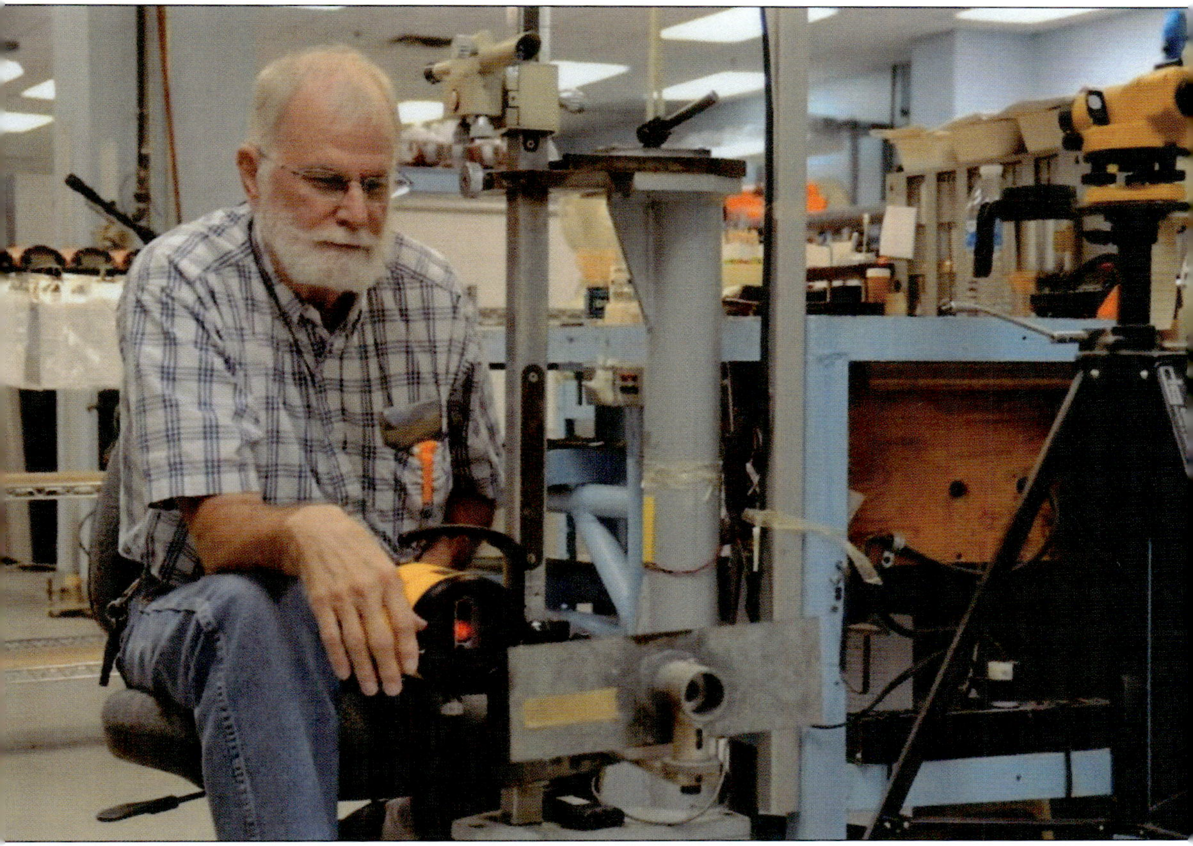

Byron Johnson, who has worked for 45 years at AGL Lasers in Jacksonville, repairs one of the lasers it sells. Engineers J.C. George and Glen Blount started the company in 1964 after inventing the first laser to be used in the construction industry for alignment purposes. (Courtesy of Jeffery Smith.)

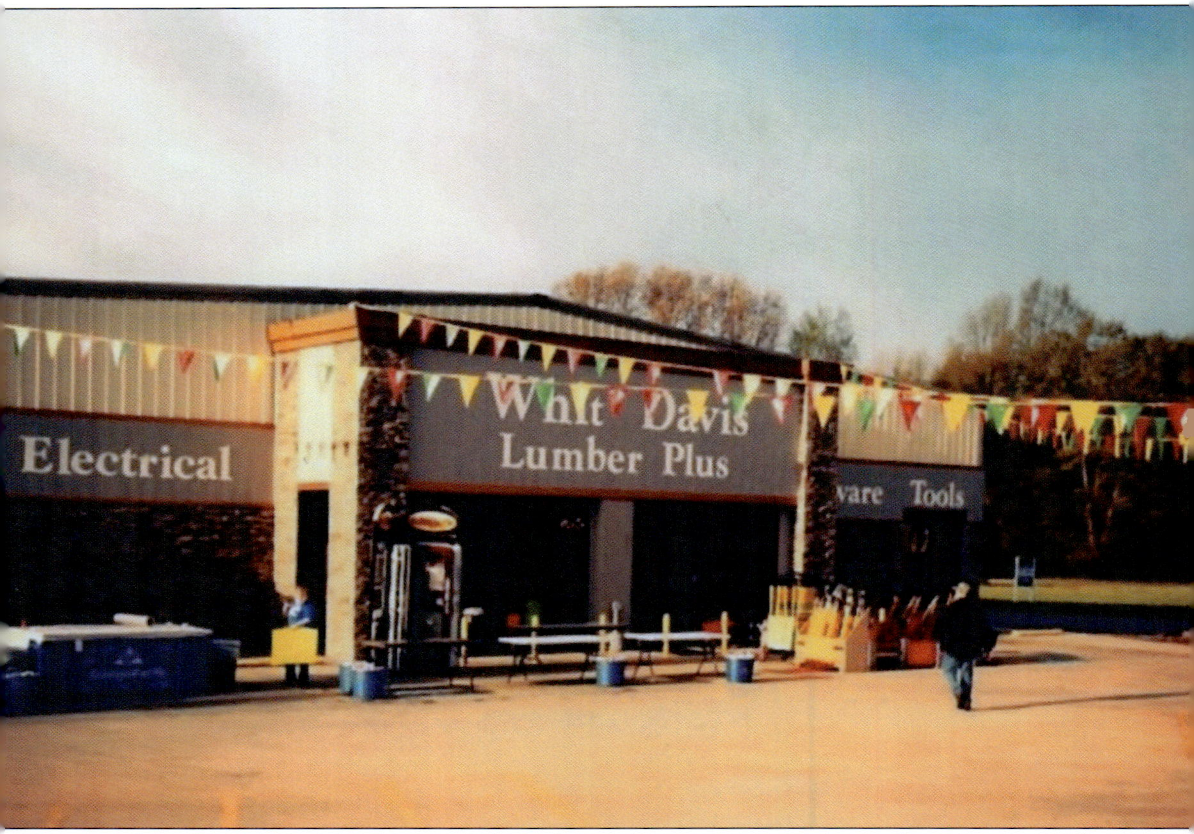

Whit Davis Lumber Company, run by Whit and Miriam Davis, was purchased in 1953 when it was known as Oliver Lumber Company. Miriam kept the books, and their son John worked there after school. He became general manager in the mid-1970s; now his sons Dan and Paul are general and operations manager, respectively. Whit Davis always said, "You have to expand to survive." (Courtesy of Whit Davis Lumber Company.)

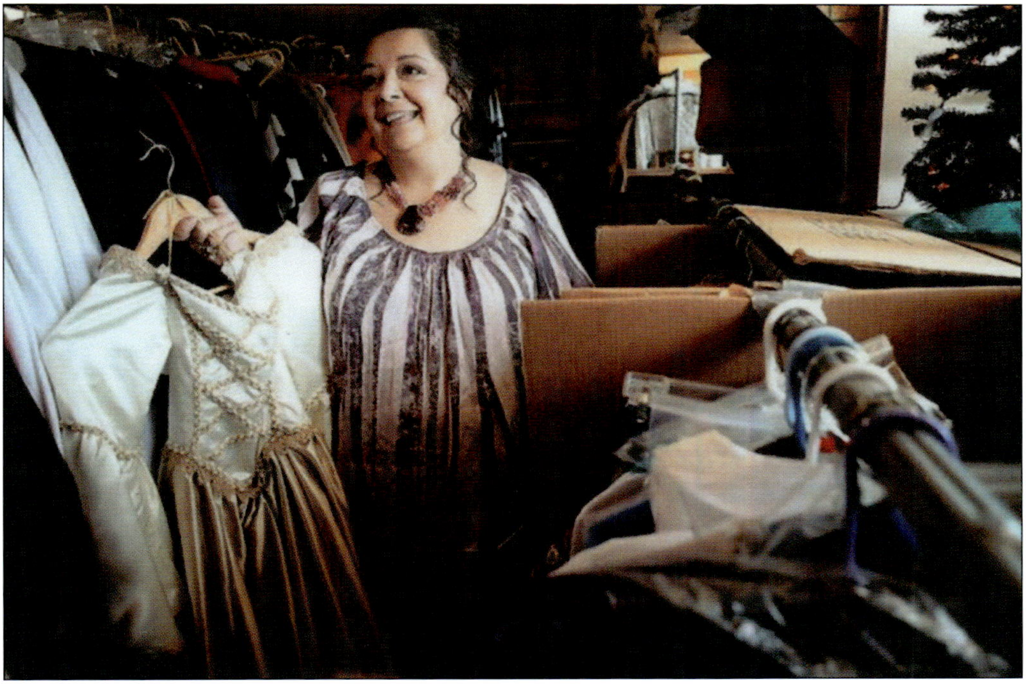

After 25 years of costuming at Costume Corner, Joe and Angie Mitchell closed the shop, but their costumes will live on. Whether they are superheroes or zombies, do not mistake them for spirits that have come to walk the streets. (Courtesy of *Three Rivers News*.)

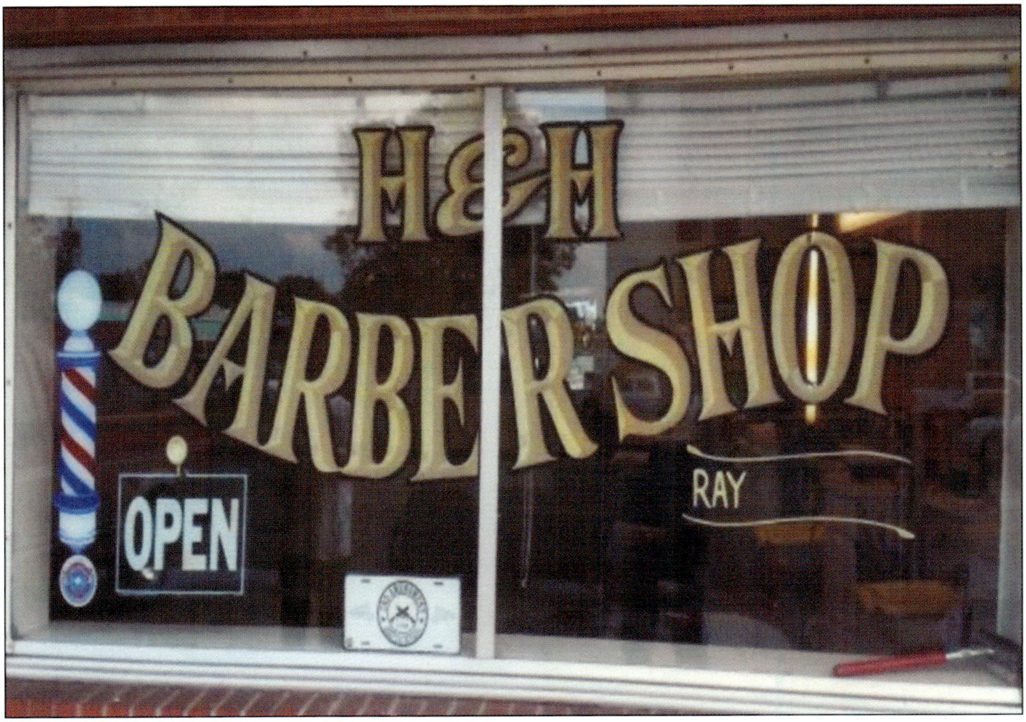

The H & H Barber Shop is located on North Bailey Street. Ray has been in business for over 25 years without having a telephone, and he only takes cash. (Courtesy of Patrick Thomas.)

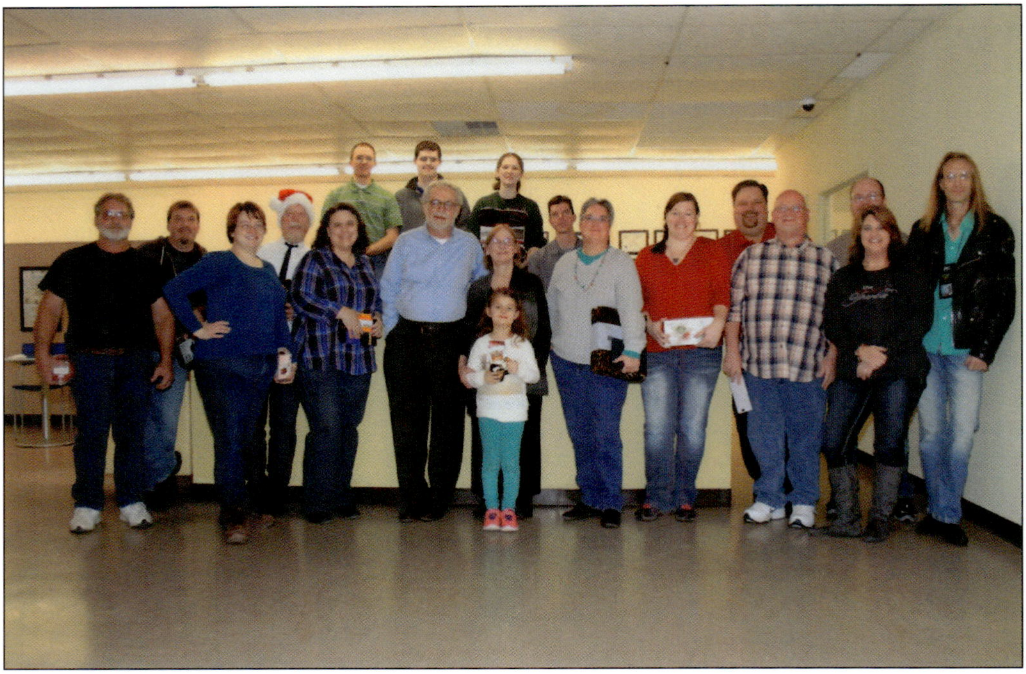

The 2014 *Leader* newspaper staff are, from left to right, Gene Johnson (plant manager), Ray Benton (sports editor), Sarah Campbell (writer), John Henderson (general manager), Tosha Churches (office manager), Thomas Alvis (accounts receivable clerk), Jacob Paddock, Haley Paddock, Garrick Feldman (publisher), Eileen Feldman (managing editor), Jeffrey Smith (writer/photographer), Lisa Tigue (graphic artist), Christy Hendricks (creative editor), Matt Robinson (publications manager), Clay Knupp (graphic artist), Graham Powell (sportswriter), Susan Swift (advertising representative), and David Scolli (photographer). (Courtesy of the *Leader*.)

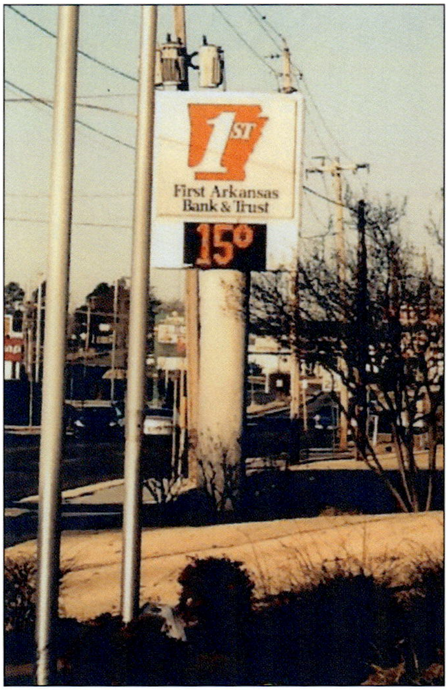

For years, this was the only sign in town informing residents of the time and temperature, and in Arkansas everyone knows the weather can change at any given moment. This sign is located on West Main Street, next to First Arkansas Bank and Trust. (Courtesy of the Jacksonville Historical District.)

Six

Parks and Recreation

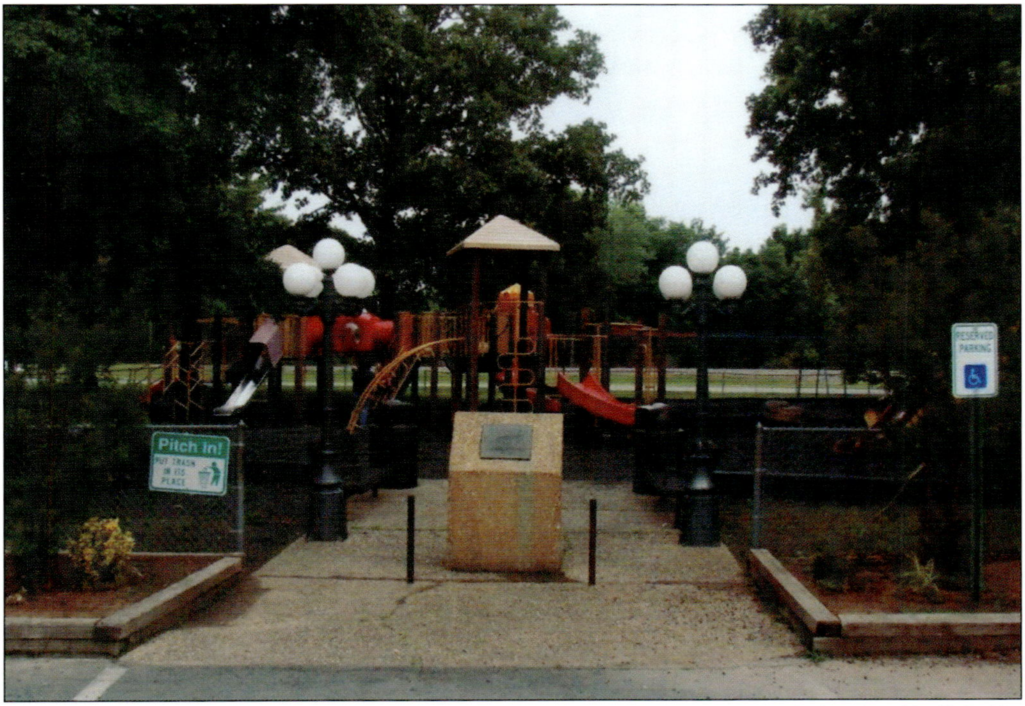

The playground is not the only thing Dupree Park has to offer; it has five lighted softball fields, a soccer and football complex, a 10-acre lake for fishing, horseshoe pit, dog park, walking trails, bike trails, and tables for family gatherings. Current park and recreation director Kevin House takes care of the parks in the town of Jacksonville. (Courtesy of the Jacksonville Parks and Recreation Department.)

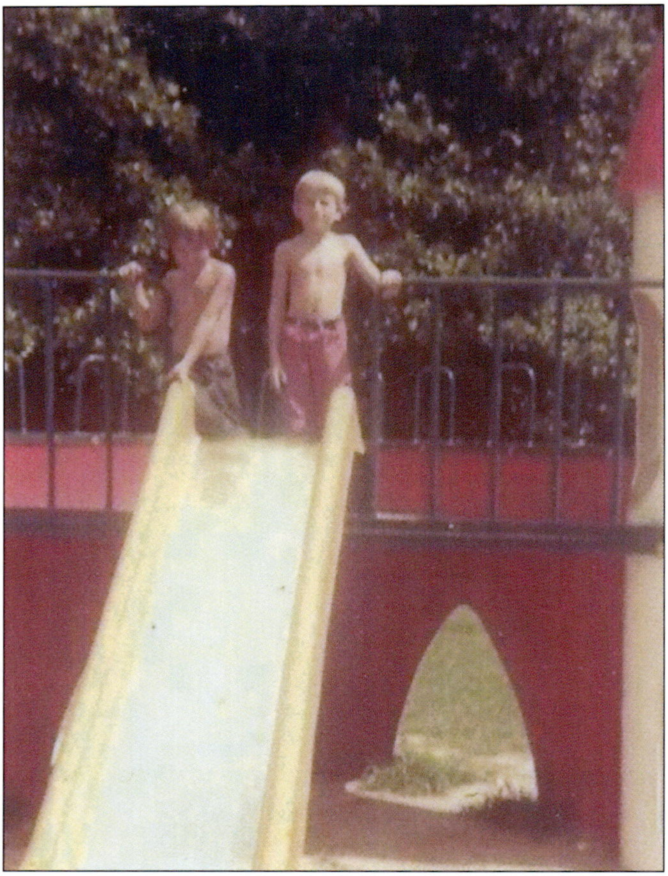

This rocket slide was at the Dupree Park playground in 1980s. Children loved to let their imaginations go wild here. A few years ago, it was taken down due to old age and replaced with another slide that keeps the children safe and happy. (Courtesy of the Jacksonville Parks and Recreation Department.)

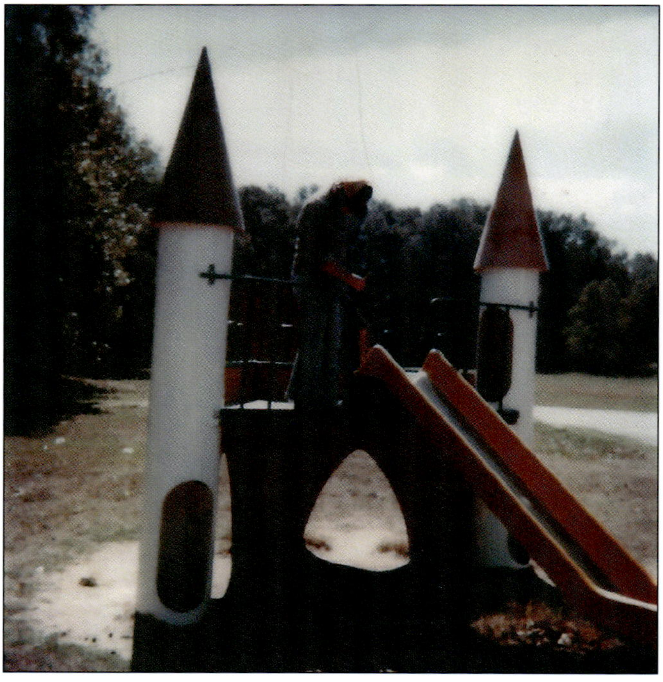

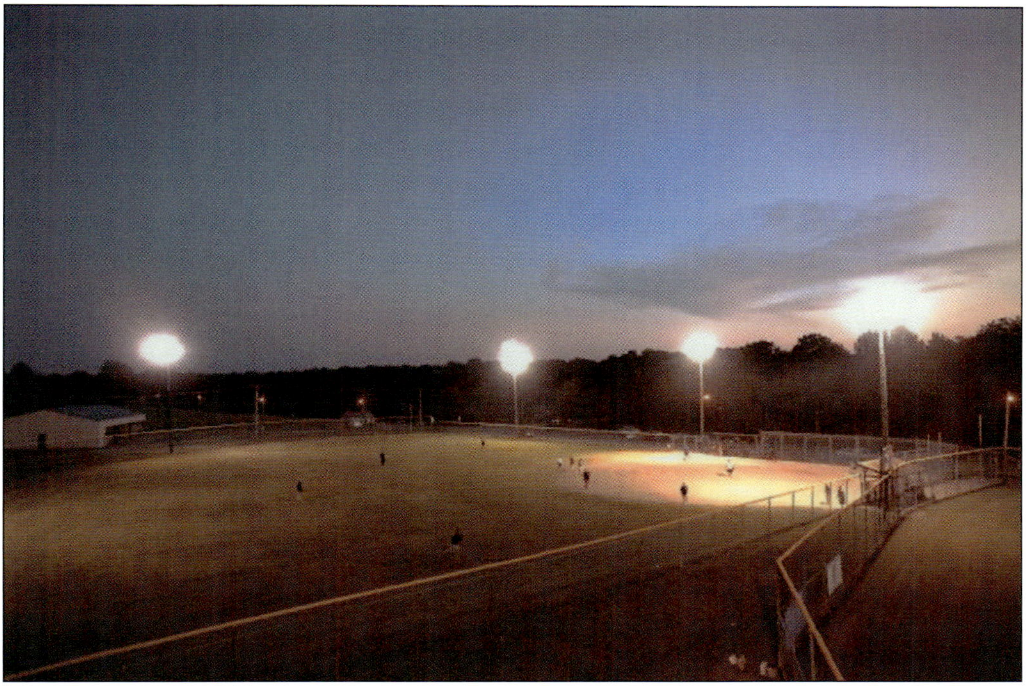

Pictured here is a baseball game held at one of the five diamonds in Dupree Park. (Courtesy of the Jacksonville Parks and Recreation Department.)

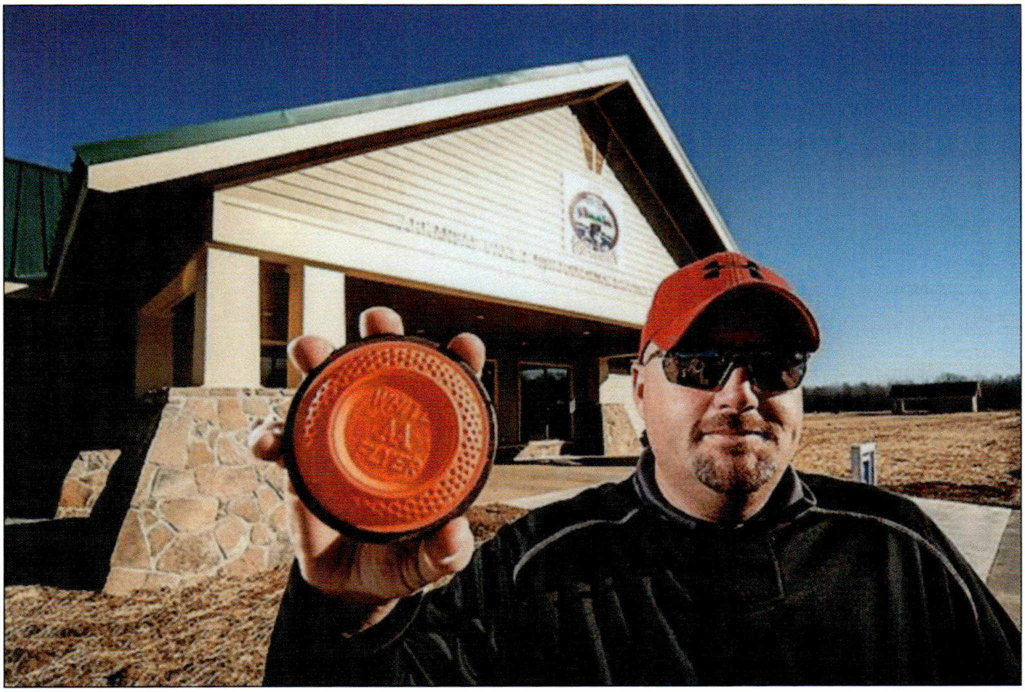

Director of Parks and Recreation Kevin House holds a skeet disc for skeet shooting. Locals have access to a brand-new, 160-acre facility in Jacksonville: the Arkansas Game and Fish Foundation Shooting Sports Complex. (Courtesy of the Jacksonville Parks and Recreation Department.)

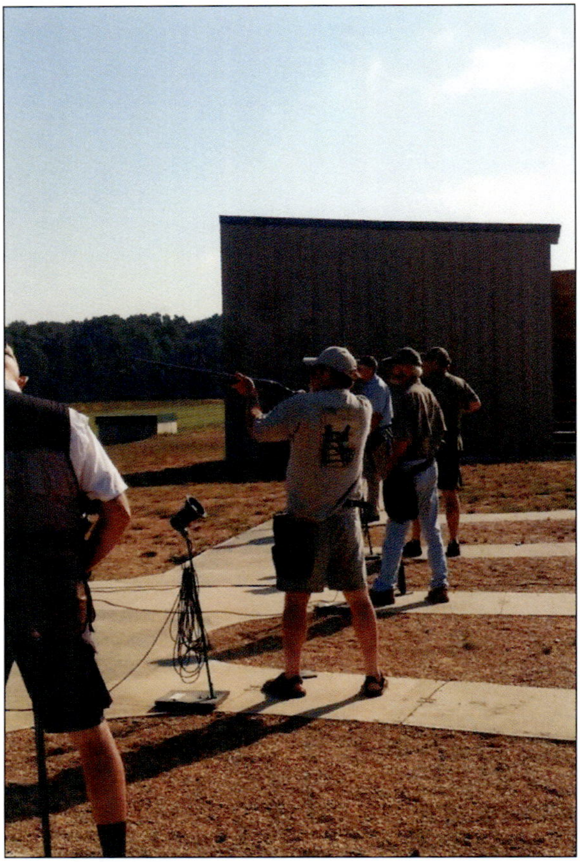

Since it opened in 2014, skeet shooting at the Arkansas Game and Fish Foundation Shooting Sports Complex has become a popular pastime. (Courtesy of the Jacksonville Parks and Recreation Department.)

Pictured here is the grand opening of the Arkansas Game and Fish Foundation Shooting Sports Complex. From left to right are Gov. Mike Beebe, Mike Knoedl, Jacksonville mayor Gary Fletcher, Ford Overton, Emon Mahoney, and John Rutledge with the air base honor guard. (Courtesy of Jeffery Smith.)

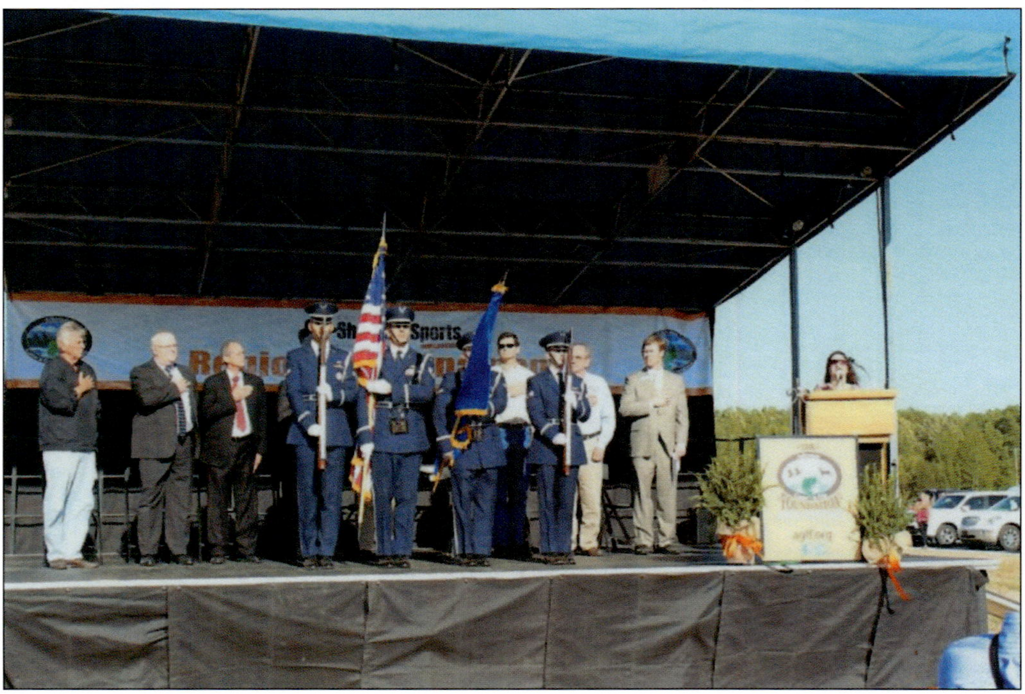

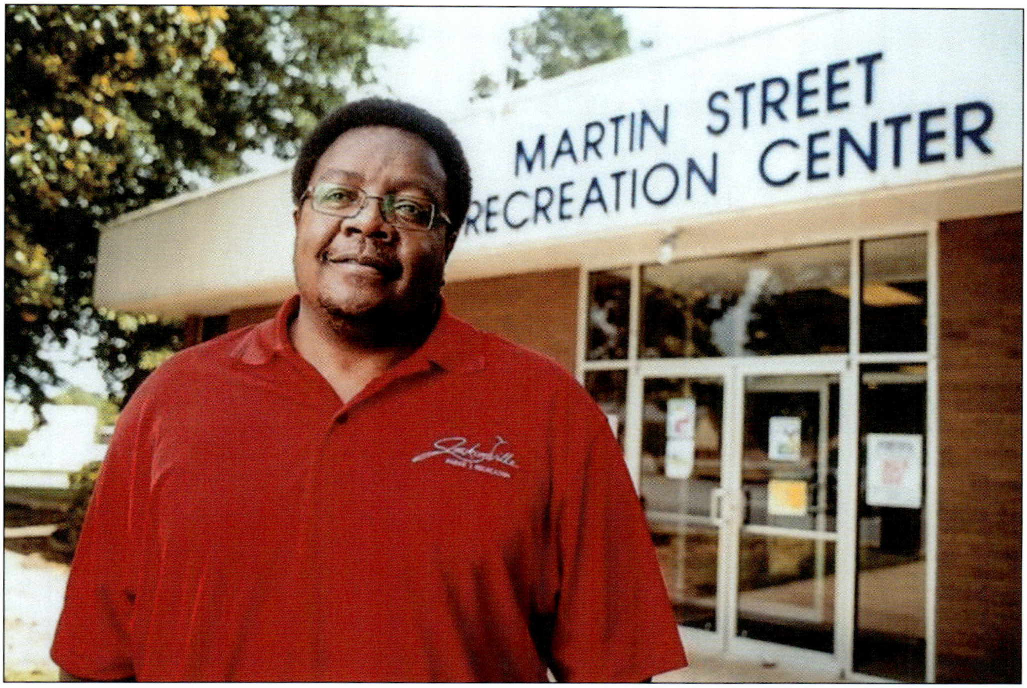

Glen Lane of Jacksonville is the coordinator for Our Club, an after-school program, and the manager of the youth center in Jacksonville. Our Club has three main components: academics, fitness, and community service. Lane has worked for the Jacksonville Parks and Recreation Department since March 1998. (Above, courtesy of Angela Spencer; below, the Jacksonville Parks and Recreation Department.)

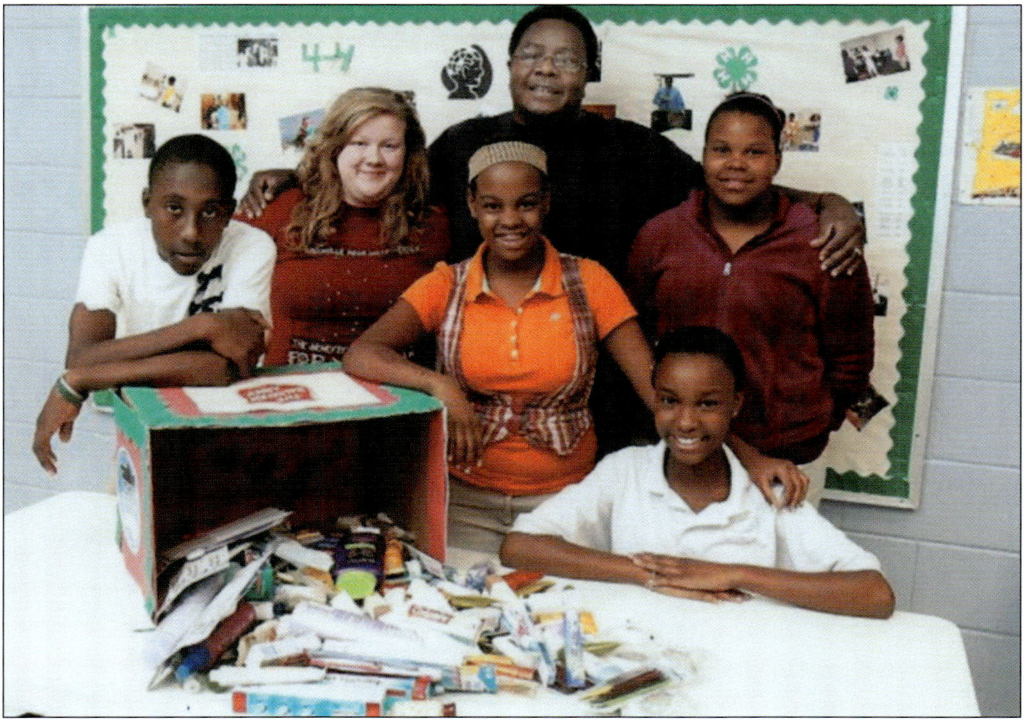

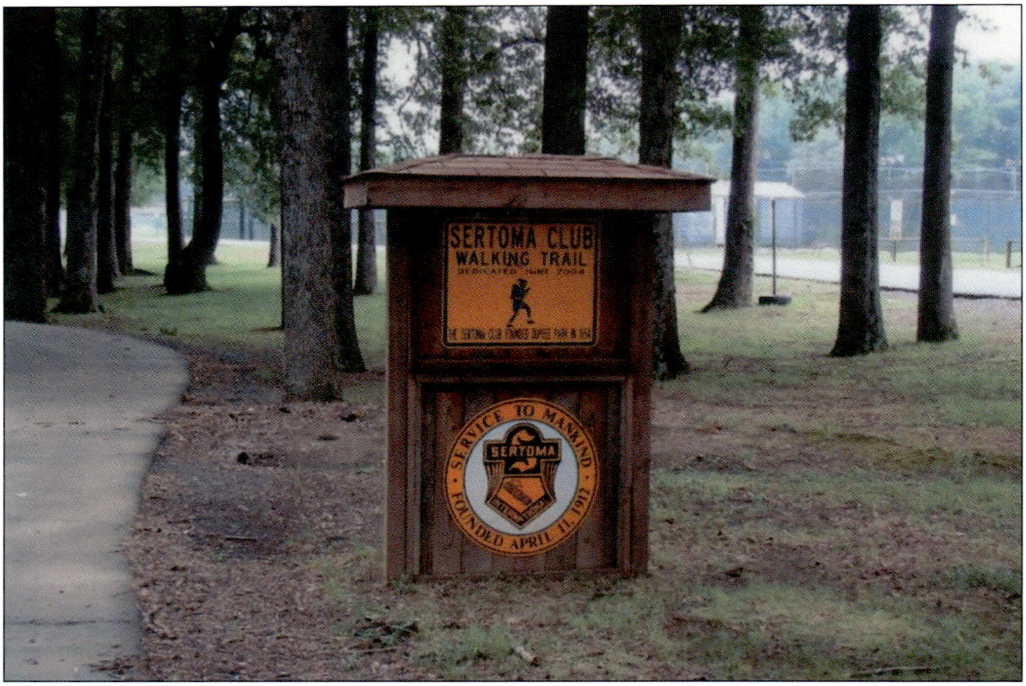

The Sertoma Club, founded on February 26, 1954, by Ron McDaniel, built this walking trail. The club was founded to aid the handicapped and help the poor. (Courtesy of the Jacksonville Historical District.)

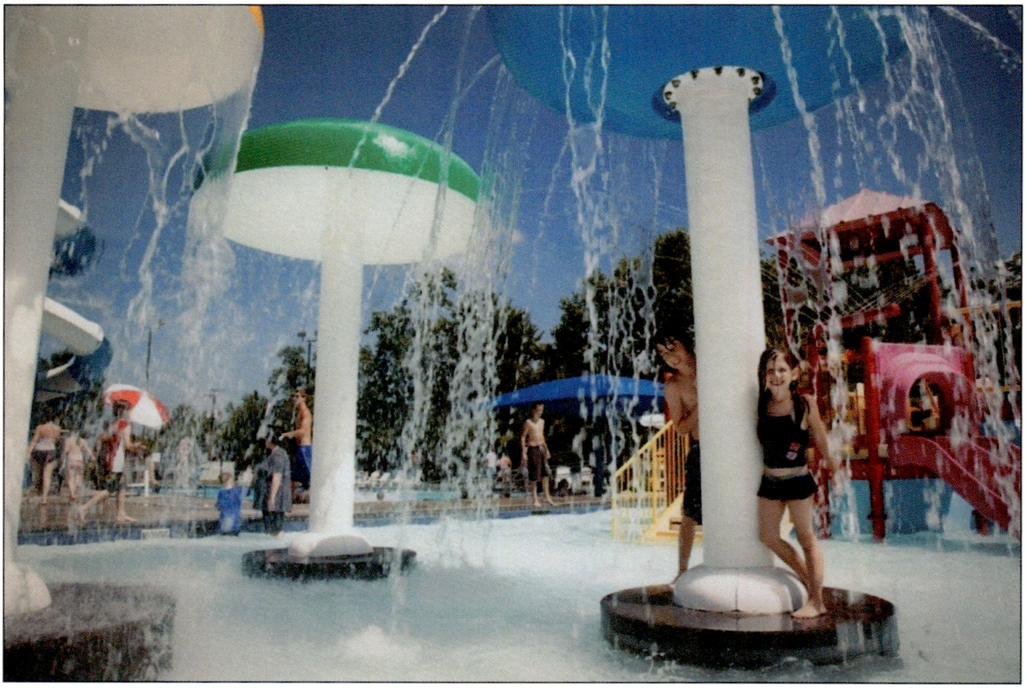

Splash Zone Water Park opened in 2005, and the park is the city's largest aquatic center, with two pools and two waterslides with a water tunnel. The umbrella raindrop water shower is designed for younger children. (Courtesy of Jill Ross.)

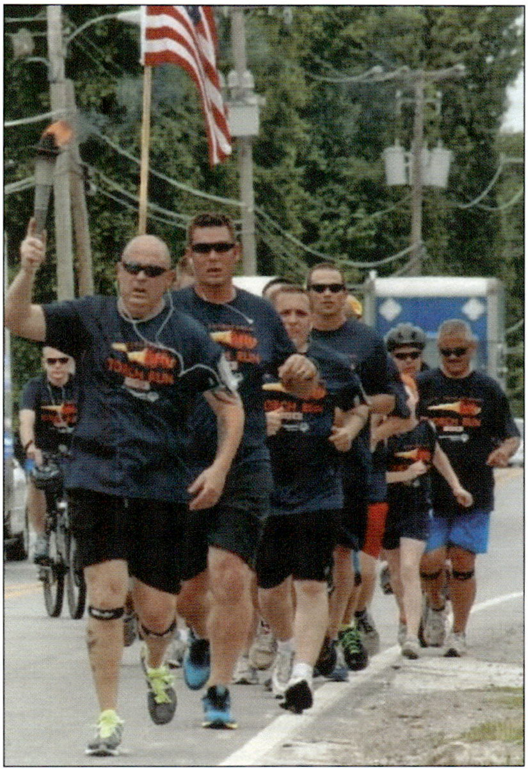

Police officer John Alberson carries the flame and officer Seth Corben carries the American flag as members of the Law Enforcement Torch Run on Main Street. The torch run is a fundraiser for the Special Olympics. (Courtesy of Jeffery Smith.)

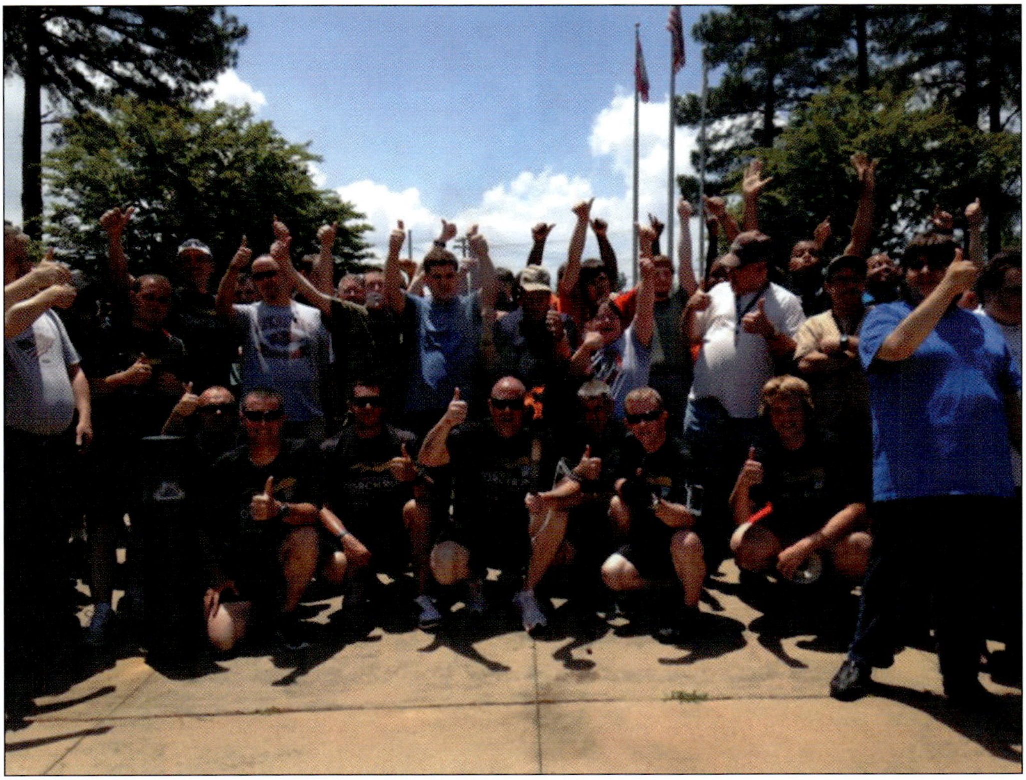

Police officers participate in the 2014 torch run, sponsored by the Jacksonville Police Department. (Courtesy of the Jacksonville Police Department.)

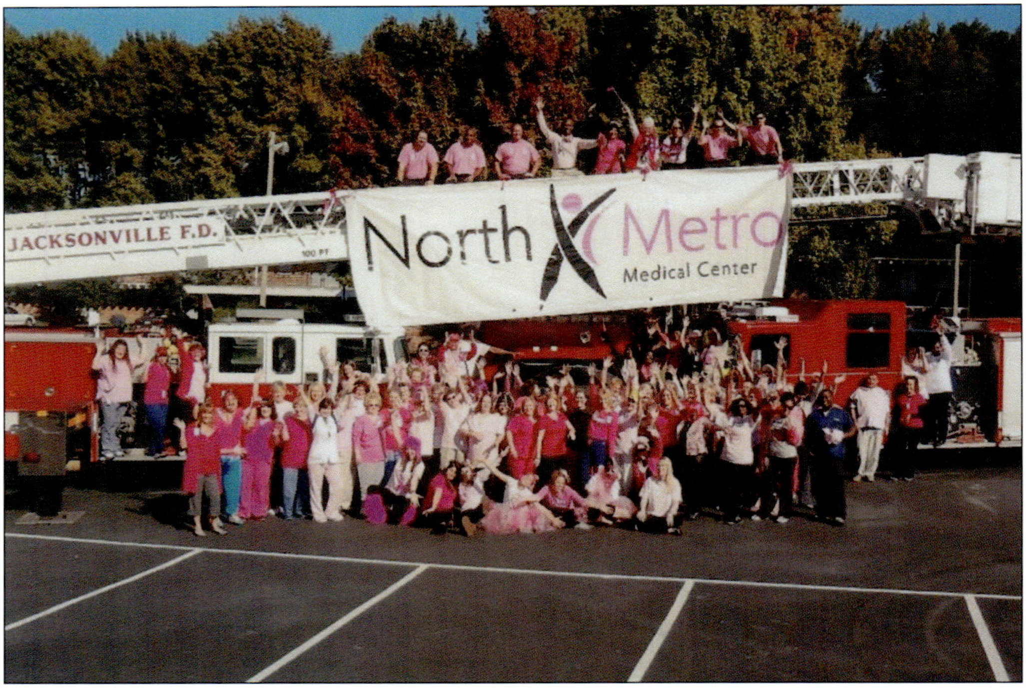

North Metro Race for the Cure is sponsored by North Metro Hospital, a small hospital with a big heart. The Jacksonville Fire Department is holding up the banner in the background. (Courtesy of the *Leader*.)

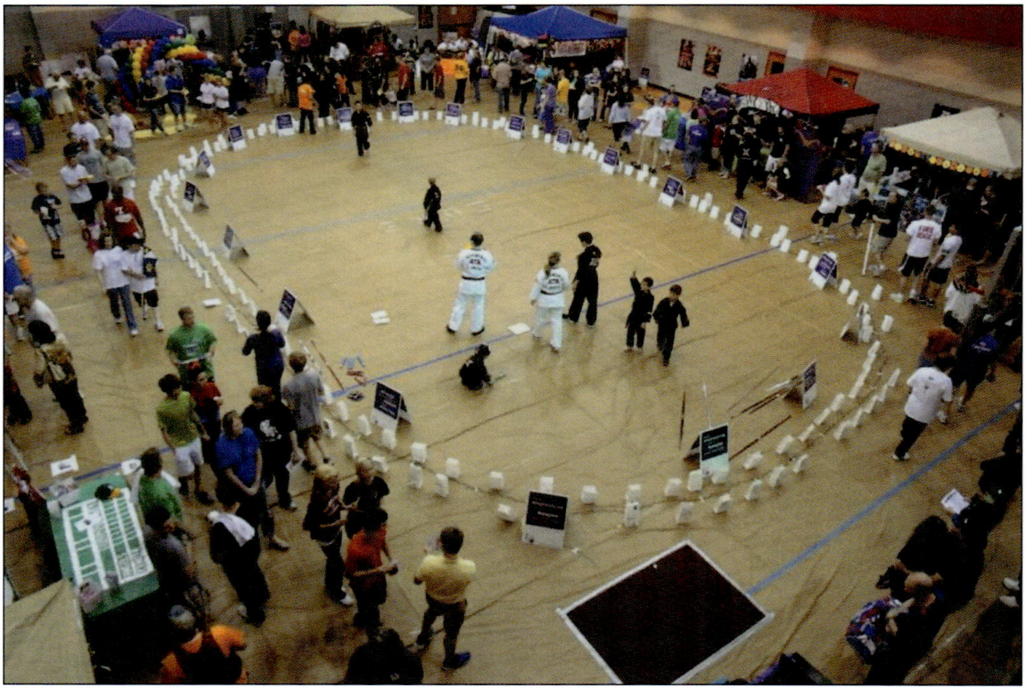

Relay for Life walkers packed the house, pounding out laps around the Jacksonville Community Center to raise funds for and awareness of cancer-fighting efforts. (Courtesy of the Jacksonville Community Center.)

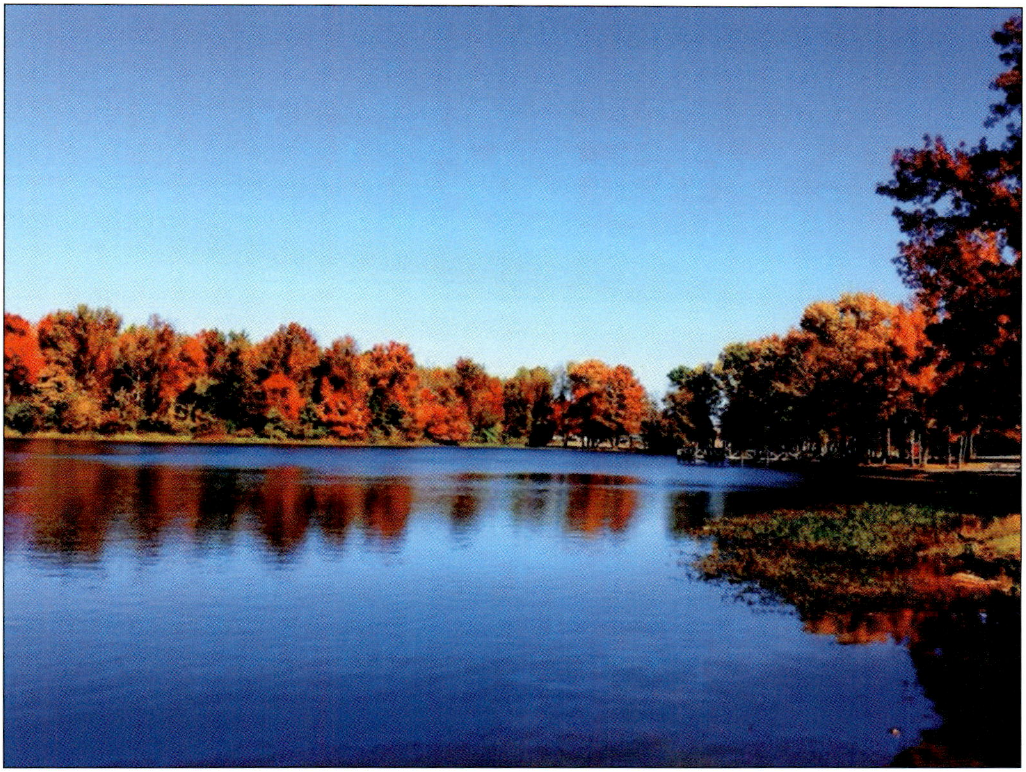

Paradise Park shows beautiful colors from Mother Nature in the fall of the year. (Courtesy of the Jacksonville Parks and Recreation Department.)

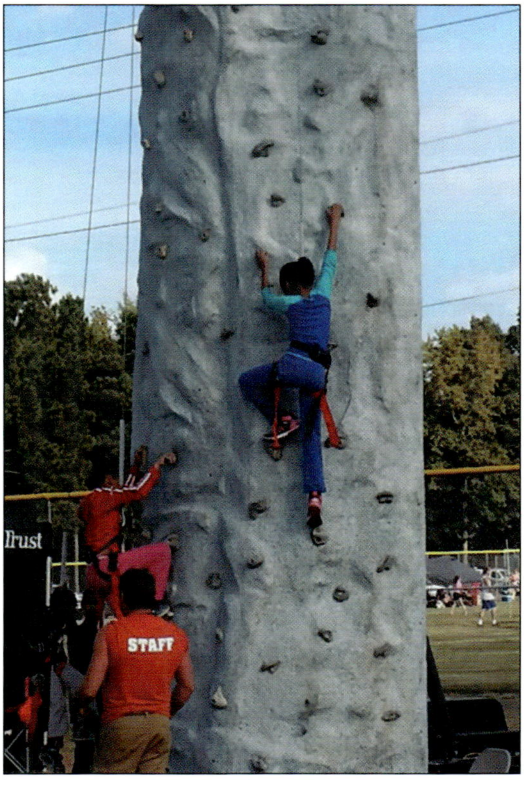

Here are a couple of youngsters testing out their skills on a climbing wall at the Jacksonville Festival that is held yearly in Dupree Park. (Courtesy of the Jacksonville Parks and Recreation Department.)

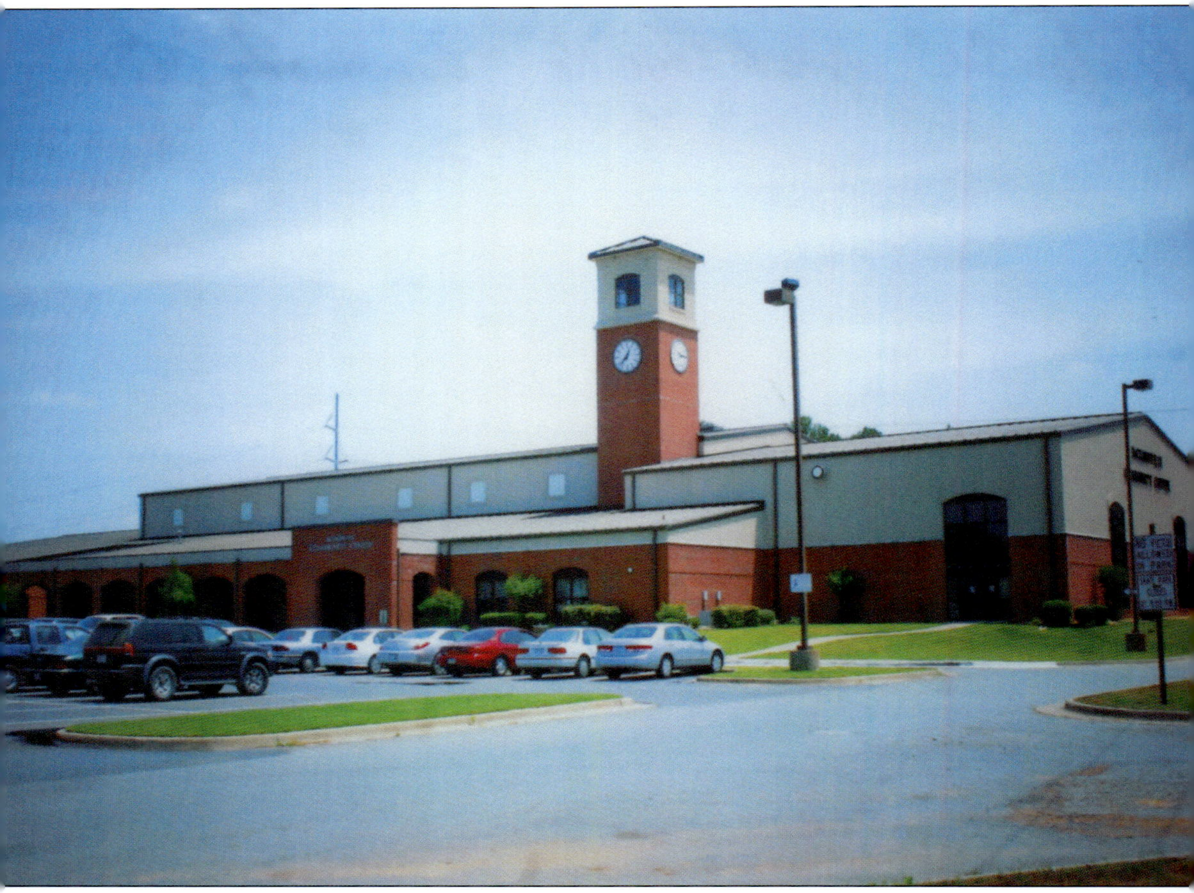

Jacksonville Community Center opened on April 10, 1995, with an award-winning, 56,000-square-foot facility that is run by the parks and recreation department. The facility offers a fitness center, gymnasium, fitness mezzanine, an aquatic area featuring a six-lane pool, a skateboard park, two racquetball courts, and both indoor and outdoor walking tracks. Workers also maintain Fireman Park on Boys Club Drive off of Graham Road, Excell Park at Southeastern Avenue and Ray Road, Galloway Park on Galloway Circle, Johnson Park on Goshen Street off of Ray Road, Paradise Park on Paradise Park Road off of Redmond Road, Stonewall Park on Berkshire Drive, Stagecoach Park on Wells Fargo Trail, and numerous other properties in the city. (Courtesy of the Jacksonville Parks and Recreation Department.)

Seven

Arts and Entertainment

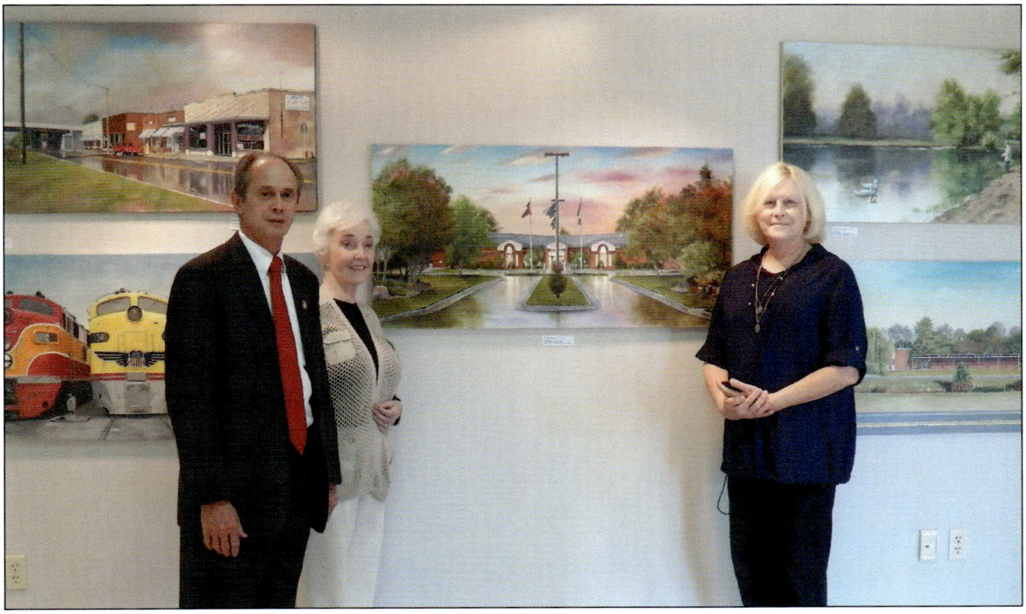

A permanent collection of RB McGrath paintings, owned by Joan Tyler Zumwalt, was installed in the lobby of Jacksonville City Hall in 2012. The collection includes a series of paintings by McGrath exhibiting historical elements and landscape scenes of the city. Local artist RB was born in the small fishing village of Branch on the island of Newfoundland to an American Air Force father and Canadian mother. The family transferred from Harmon Air Force Base to Little Rock Air Force Base in 1965. RB was 14 years old when they moved, and the family has remained in Jacksonville since. RB attended Jacksonville High School. After traveling for several years, she returned to take up residence in town, opening a salon and gallery in 1995 in the historical district. An avid amateur musician, McGrath also plays violin and cello as part of a seven-member string ensemble and is a prolific supporter of visual arts and music education. The artist's long-term goal has been the creation of a center for the arts for the city that will house a museum of fine art with a permanent collection, an art school, music school, and performance hall. (Courtesy of RB McGrath.)

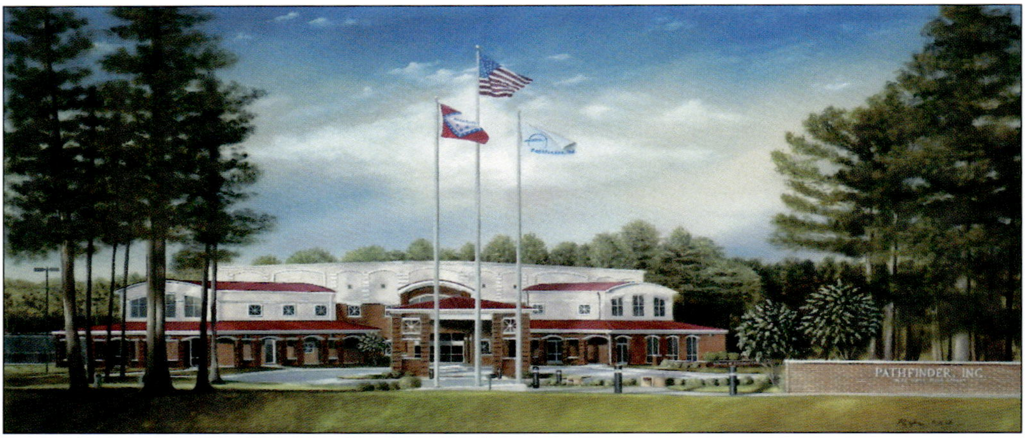

This portrait, an oil on canvas by McGrath, is called *The Reynolds*. Part of the Joan Tyler Zumwalt collection, it is now on permanent exhibit at the Pathfinder Administration Building, located at corner of West Main Street and Redmond Road. (Courtesy of RB McGrath.)

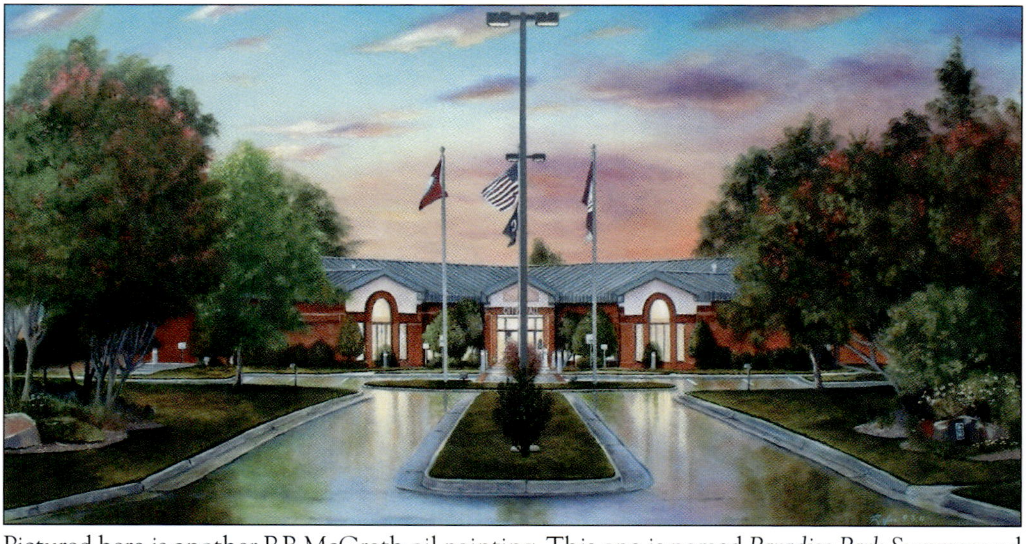

Pictured here is another RB McGrath oil painting. This one is named *Paradise Park Summer* and on display in city hall. (Courtesy of RB McGrath.)

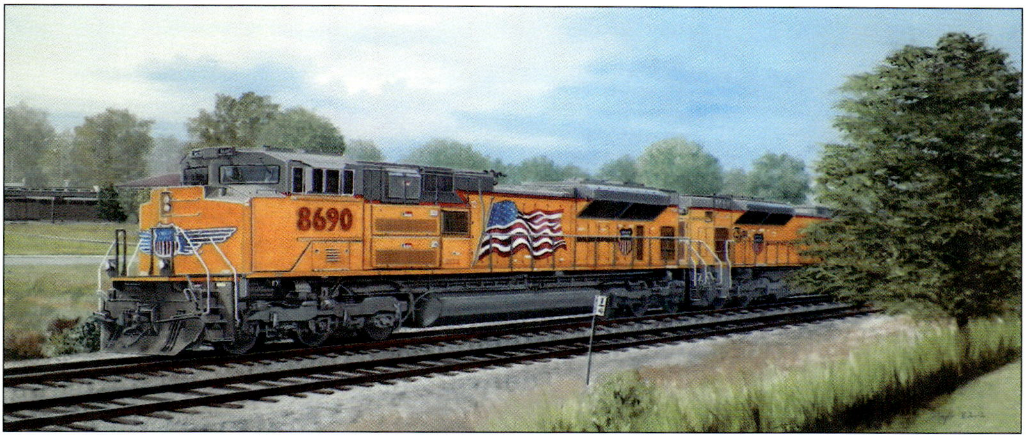

The Union Pacific Train No. 8690 was painted by RB McGrath in 2013, and it is now on exhibit in the Pathfinder Administration Building. (Courtesy of RB McGrath.)

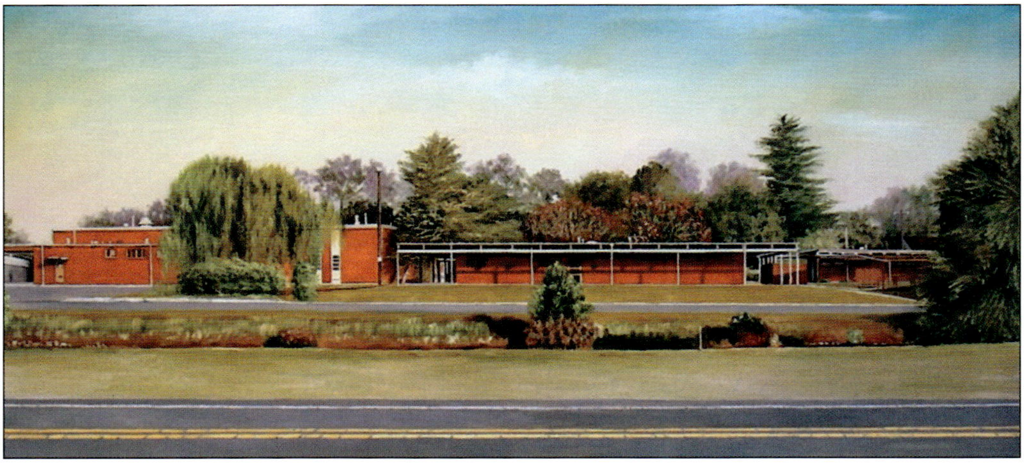

Pictured here is the back side of the Jacksonville Elementary School facing the railroad tracks at sunset. The painting is part of the Joan Tyler Zumwalt collection. (Courtesy of RB McGrath.)

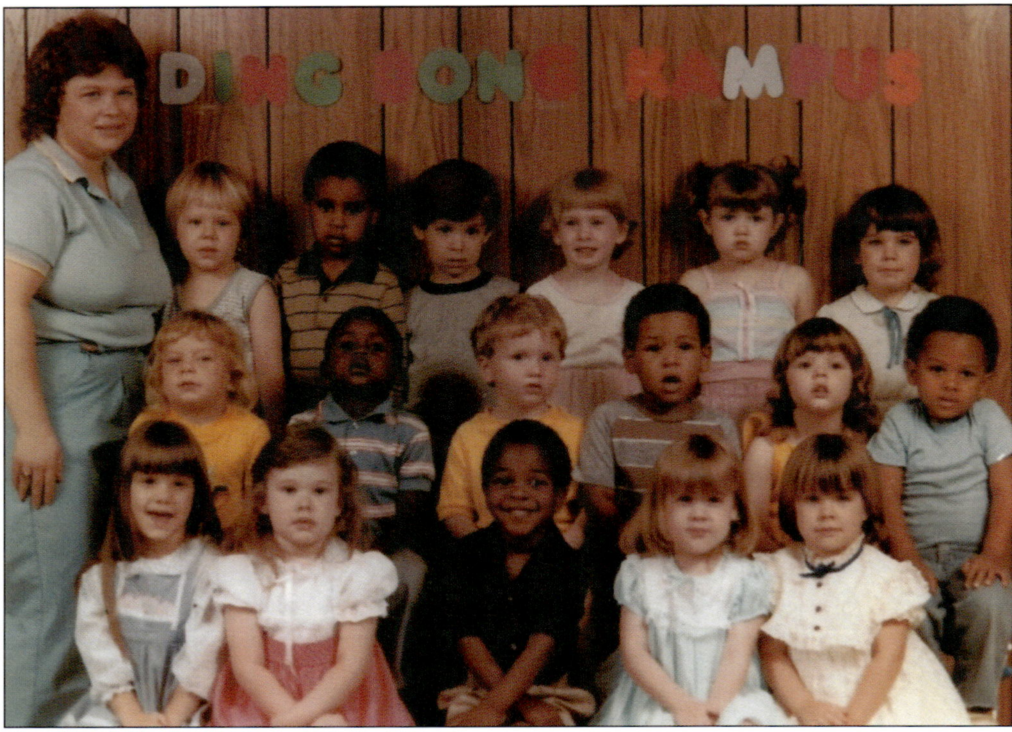

Wanda Sanders is pictured in the 1980s with her toddler-aged students at Ding Dong Campus Day Care. She went to work there in high school, when Joan Ryan was the director and Alice Schmitt was the owner. (Courtesy of Wanda Sanders.)

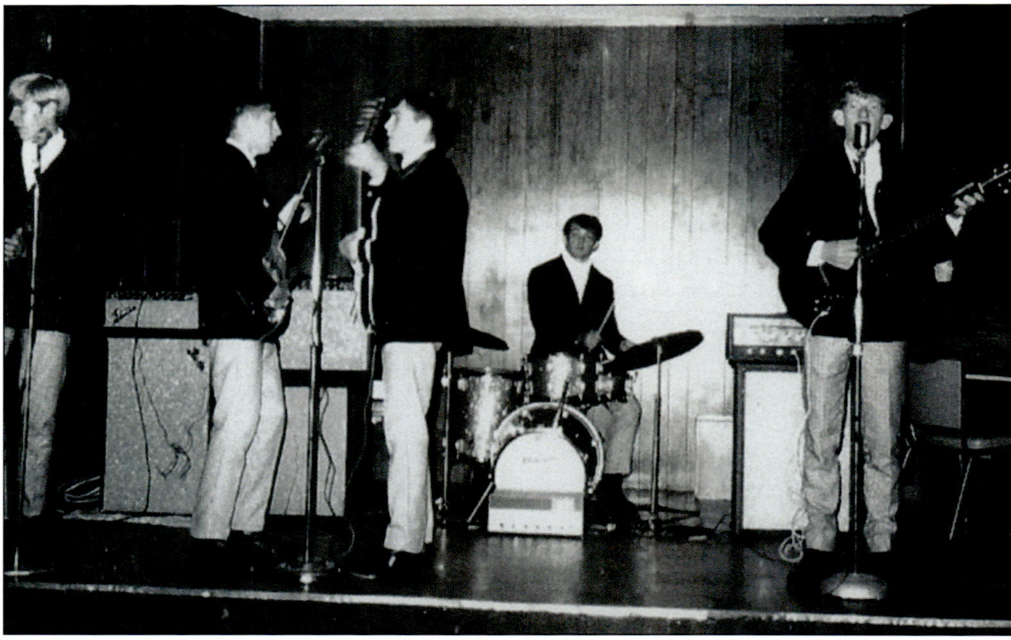

The Lost Souls began as a four-piece combo in 1966: Fil Griggs on guitar and vocals, Mike Petray on lead guitar and vocals, Danny Goldman on drums, and Bob Whitley on bass. (Courtesy of the Jacksonville Historical District.)

Jacksonville Guitar owner Steve Evans (front) is flanked by his longtime employees, from left to right, Bob Appleby, Bobby Tanner, and Bruce Maddox. This photograph, taken in 2015, marks 40 years in business. Evans entered the retailing business in 1975 at the age of 18 by opening the Jacksonville Guitar Center. (Courtesy of Steve Evans.)

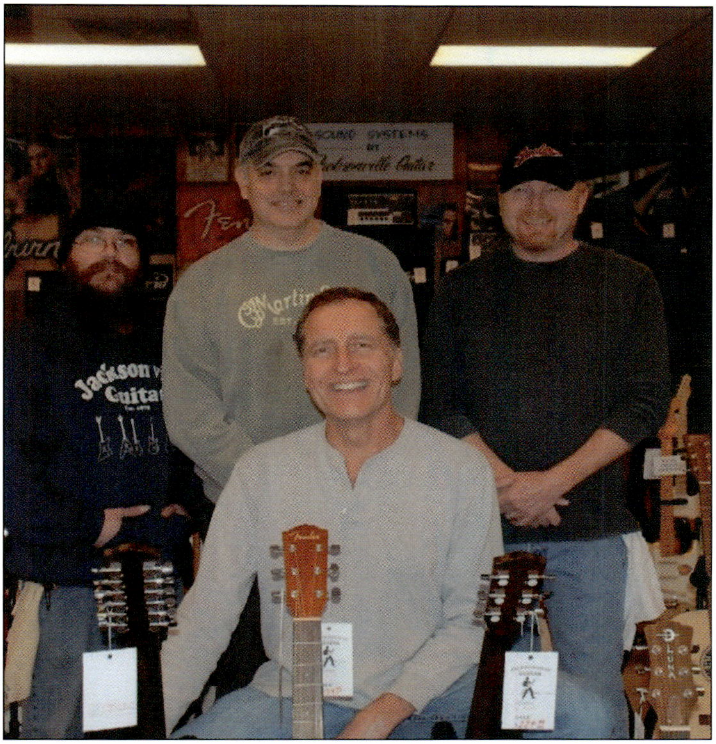

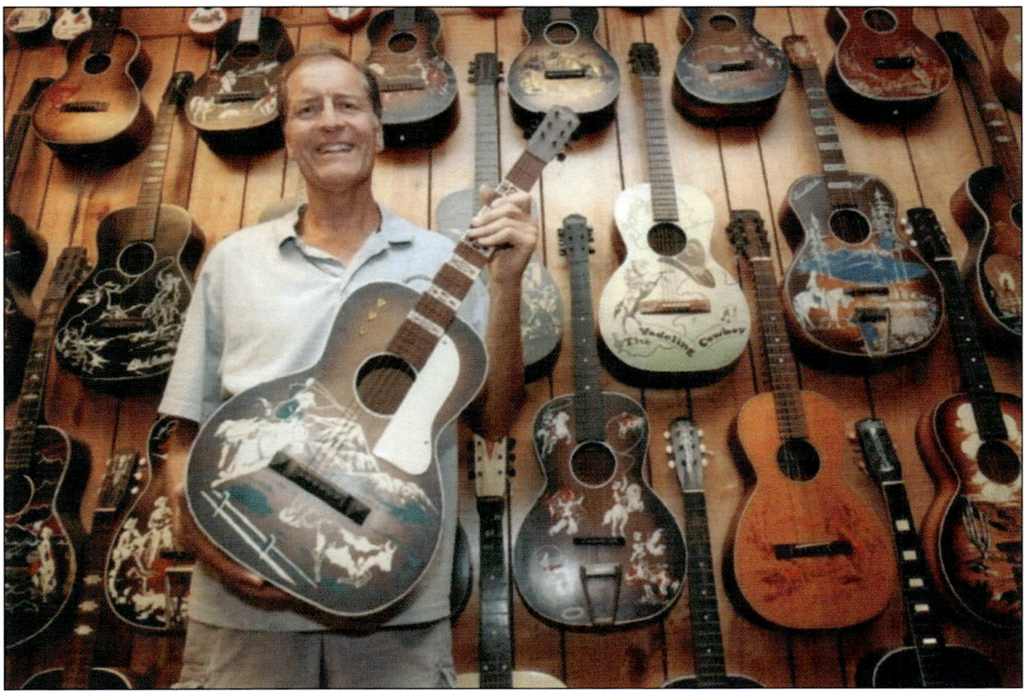

Jacksonville Guitar owner Steve Evans holds one of his cowboy guitars from his extensive collection, which is displayed at his shop at 1105 Burman Drive. Evans is considered the foremost expert on cowboy guitars, which were popular from the 1930s to 1960s. (Courtesy of the Jacksonville Historical District.)

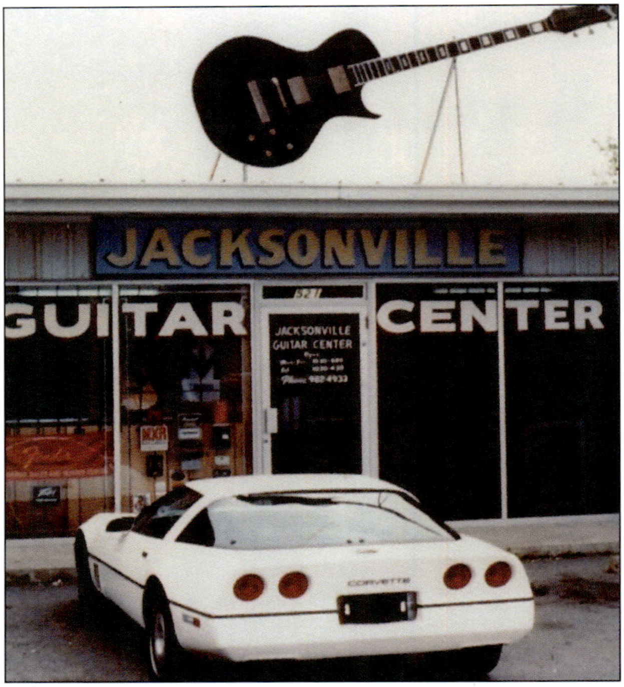

Jacksonville Guitar Center was located at 521 Dupree Drive from 1975 until 1986, when it moved to a new building constructed by Steve Evans on 1105 Burman Drive. Below, in 1975, Les Evans built this large guitar for the top of son Steve Evans's new store Jacksonville Guitar. It was 4 feet by 12 feet, and he cut out pieces of aluminum and nailed them in place to replicate the frets, used baby-food jars painted gold inside for control knobs, the pickups and bridge were made of wood, and strings were plastic-covered cables. (Courtesy of Steve Evans.)

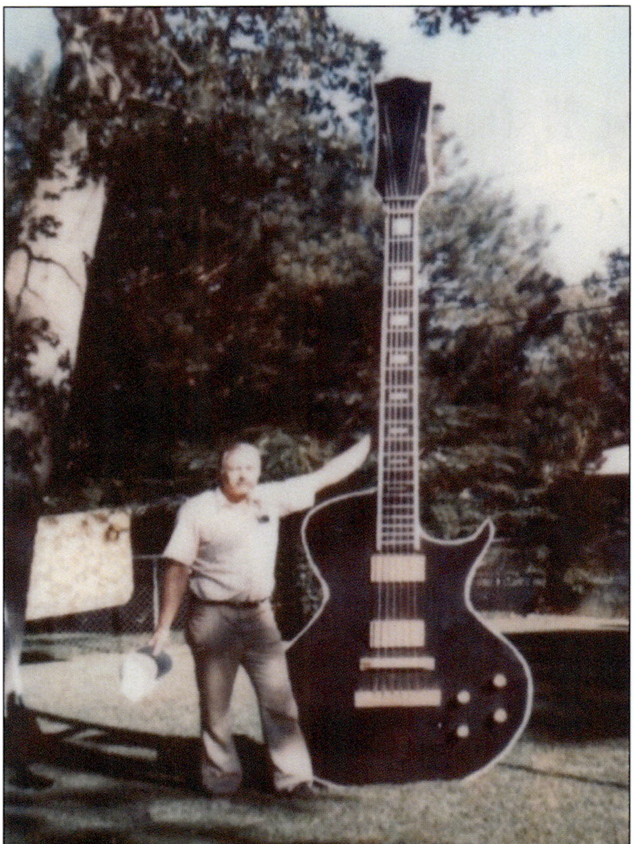

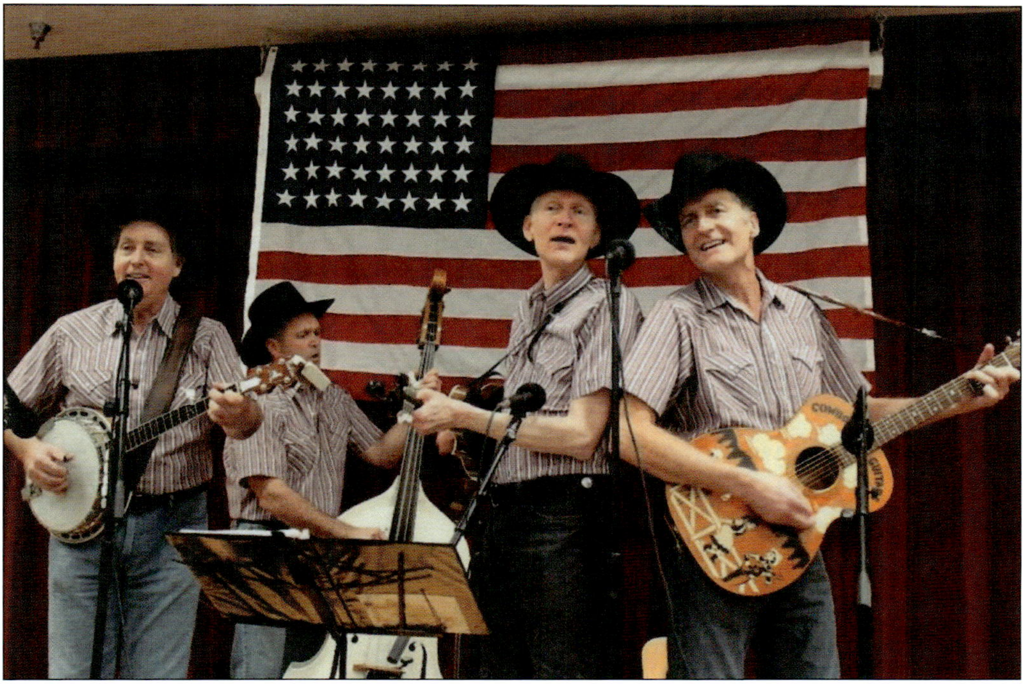

The Bluegrass Bombers perform during the Jacksonville Museum of Military History's annual fundraiser dinner at the community center. From left to right are John Lee (banjo), David Durham (upright bass), David Evans (fiddle), and Steve Evans (guitar). (Courtesy of Steve Evans.)

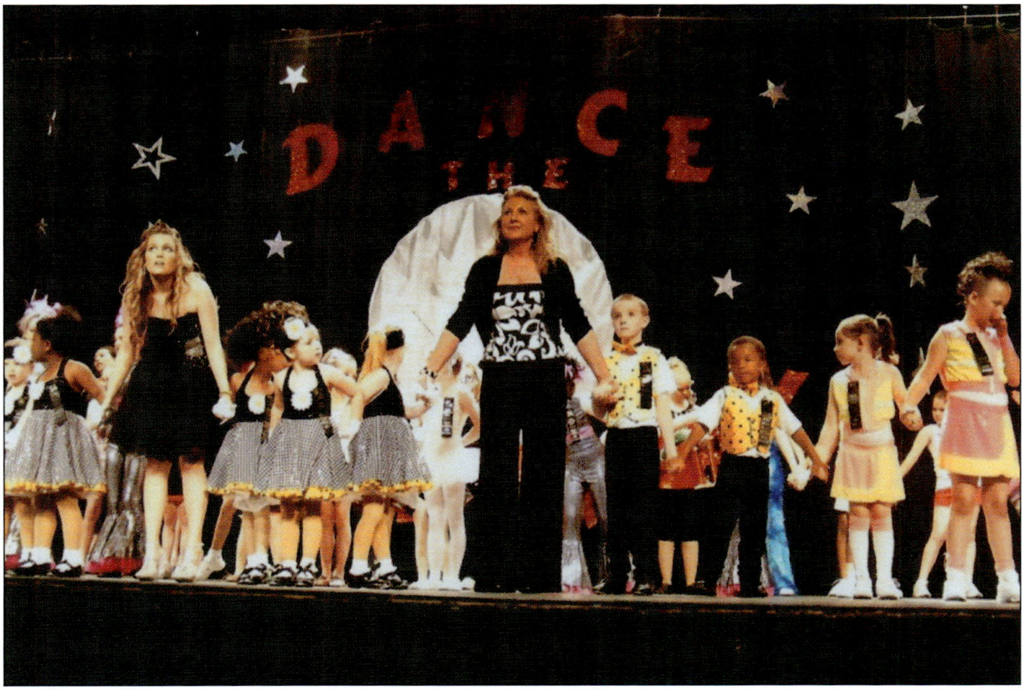

Sharon Boyd began teaching at age 12 for her dance teacher, Charlotte Peacock, and later started her own business at the age of 18. Sharon's Dance Studio has been in Jacksonville for 38 years; pictured here are some of her students after a performance. (Courtesy of Sharon's Dance Studio.)

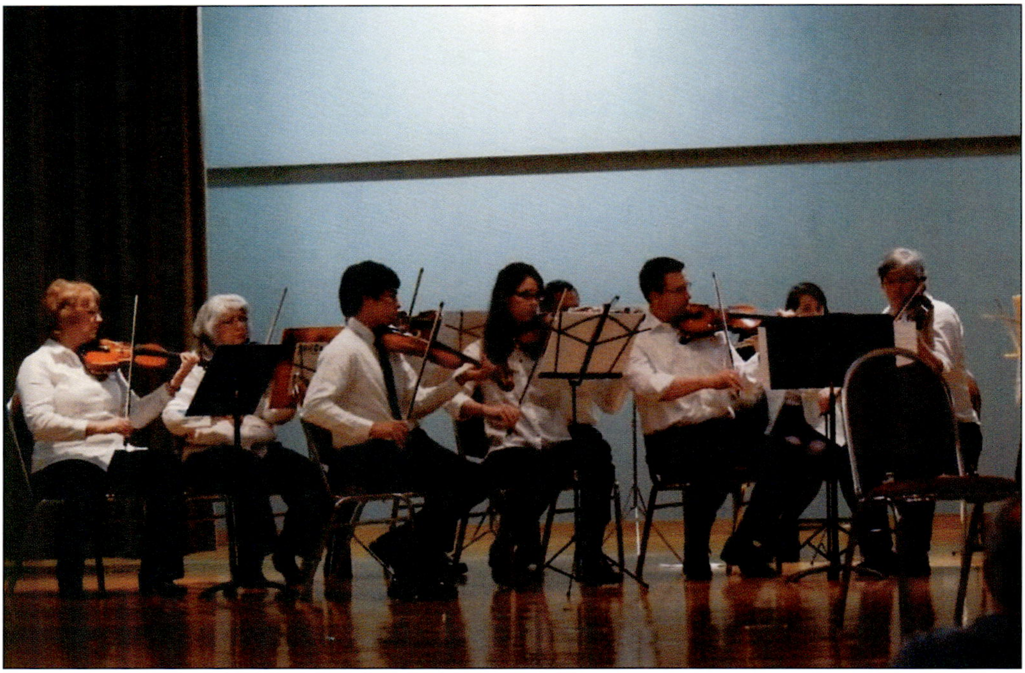

These two images depict the string section of the Jacksonville Community Orchestra at a 2013 event held at the Jacksonville Community Center. (Authors' collection.)

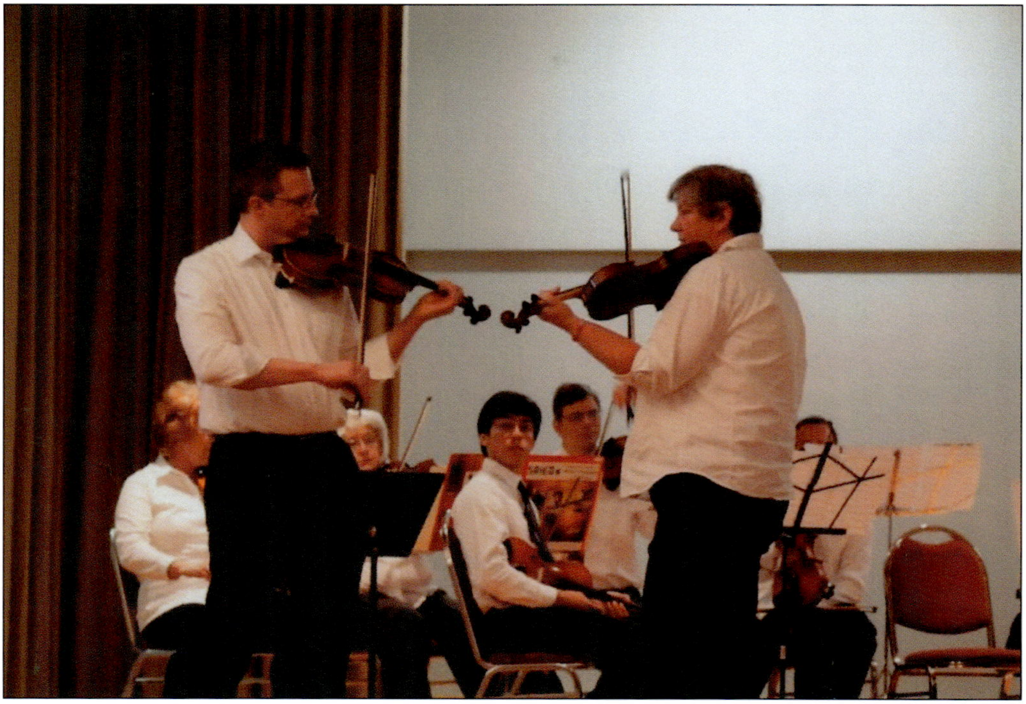

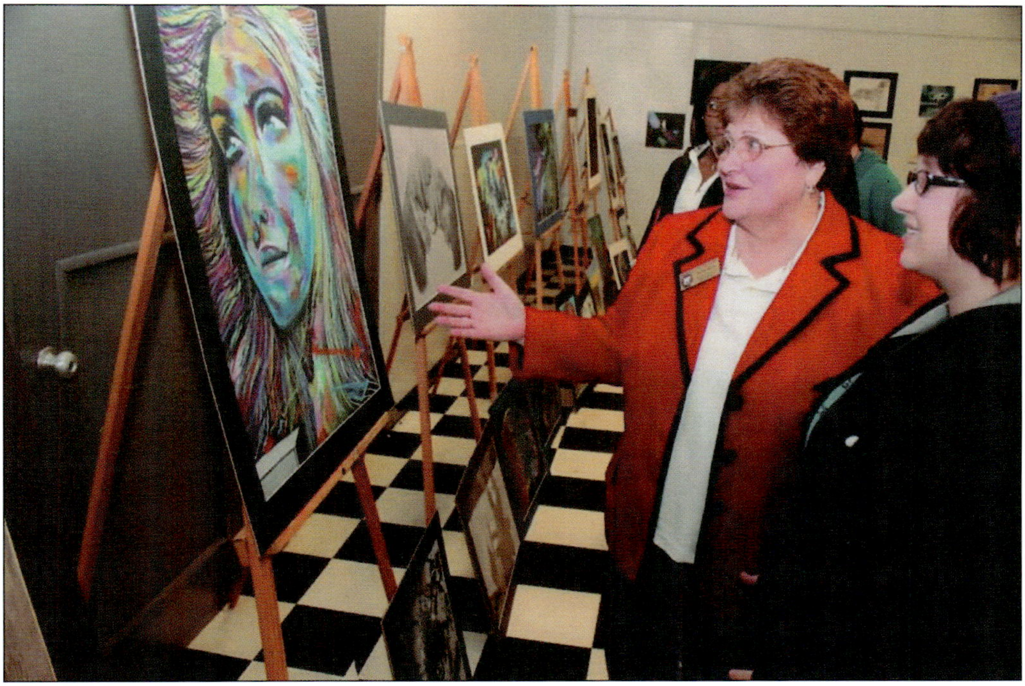

Brianna Mashburn (right), a Jacksonville High School 10th-grader and coauthor of this book, discusses her artwork with her mother, Ald. Barbara Mashburn, at the third annual For the Love of the Arts event in 2013. This painting sold for $60. (Courtesy of Jeffery Smith.)

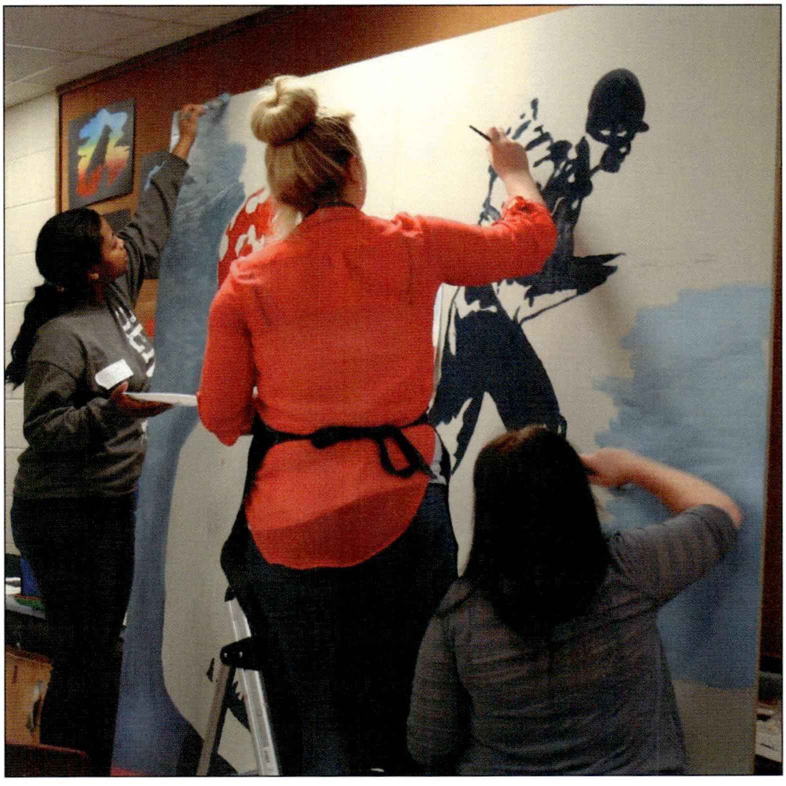

A town mural is being painted by Jacksonville High School students to be placed on the side of building in town for everyone to admire. (Courtesy of Jacksonville High School.)

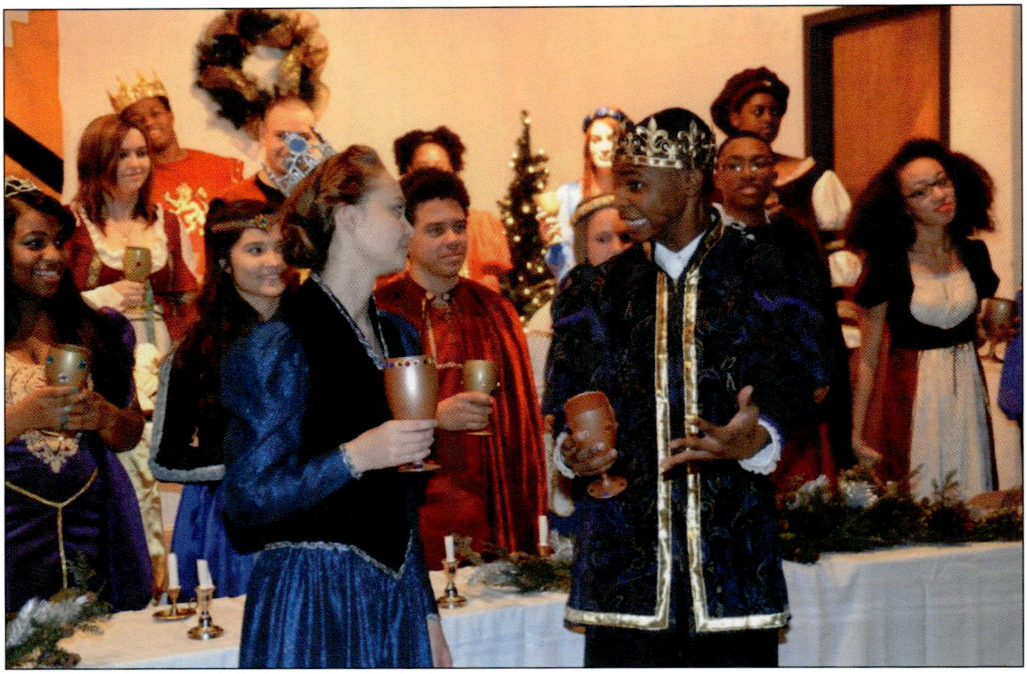

Queen Hannah Moler and King Jamal Bell from Jacksonville High School lead the choir in a toast at the 30th Madrigal Dinner, an annual event. (Courtesy of Sarah Campbell.)

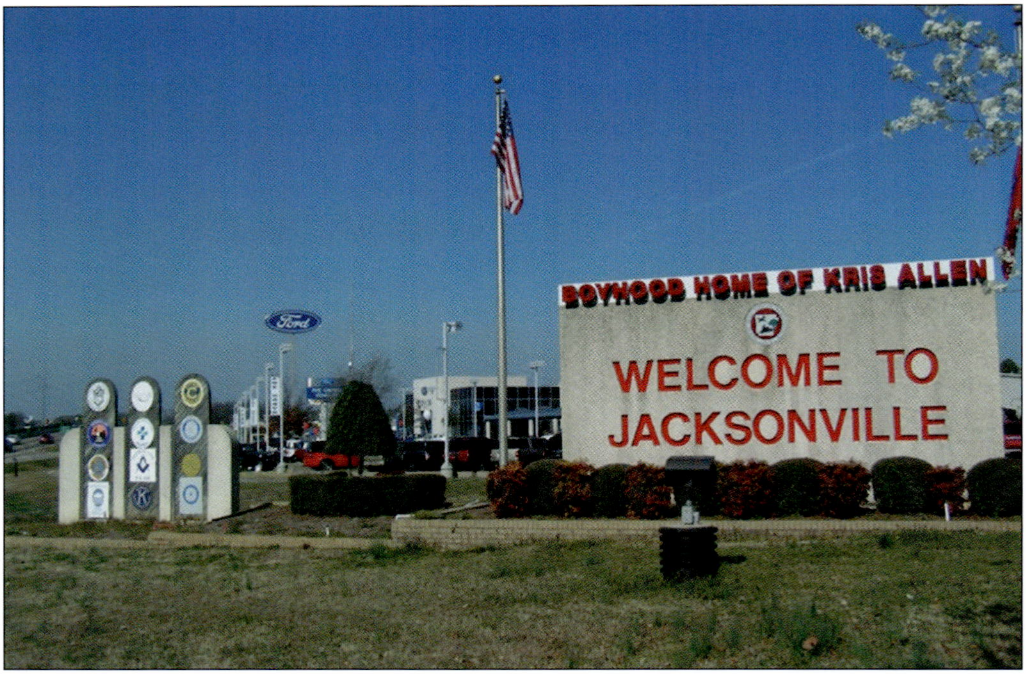

The "Welcome to Jacksonville" sign was erected at the Main Street exit from Freeway 67/167. The following contributed to construction: Bill Canino-Rendering (architect), Tommy Jameson (contractor), Arkansas Precast Corporation, Jacksonville Chamber of Commerce City Enrichment Committee, Jameson Ladd (chairman), Mayor James Reid, and the Jacksonville Jaycees. (Courtesy of Jill Ross.)

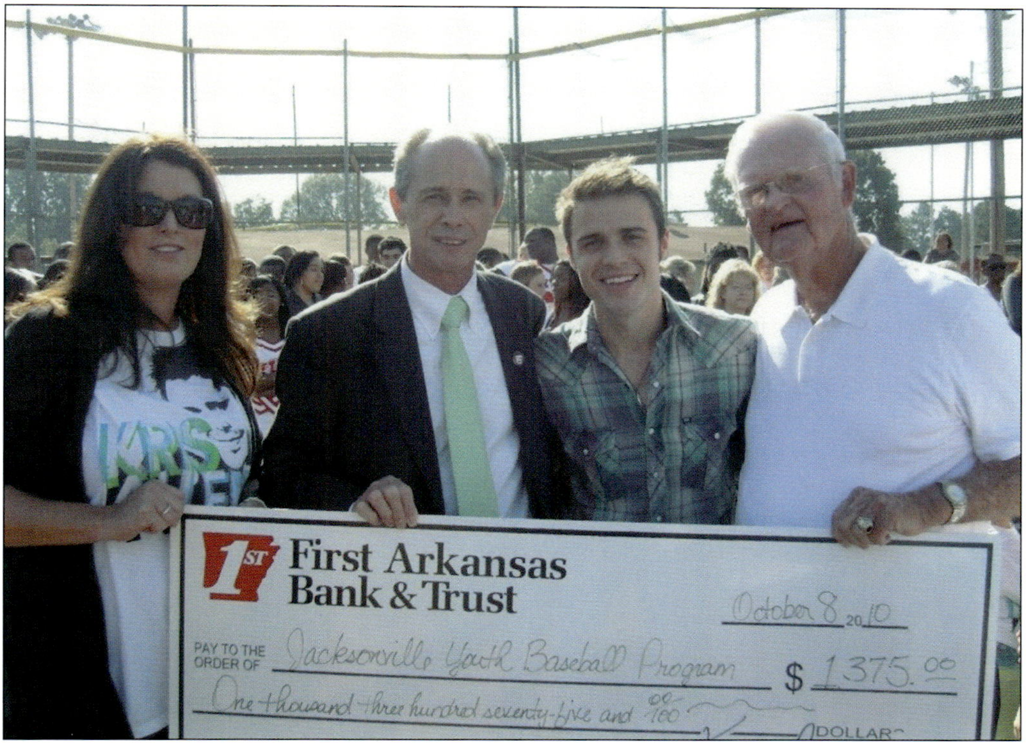

Kris Allen (above) poses with a check for the youth baseball program and shakes hands and greets schoolchildren (below) after his win on *American Idol* at Excell Park. Allen is a hometown boy from Jacksonville. (Courtesy of the Jacksonville Historical District.)

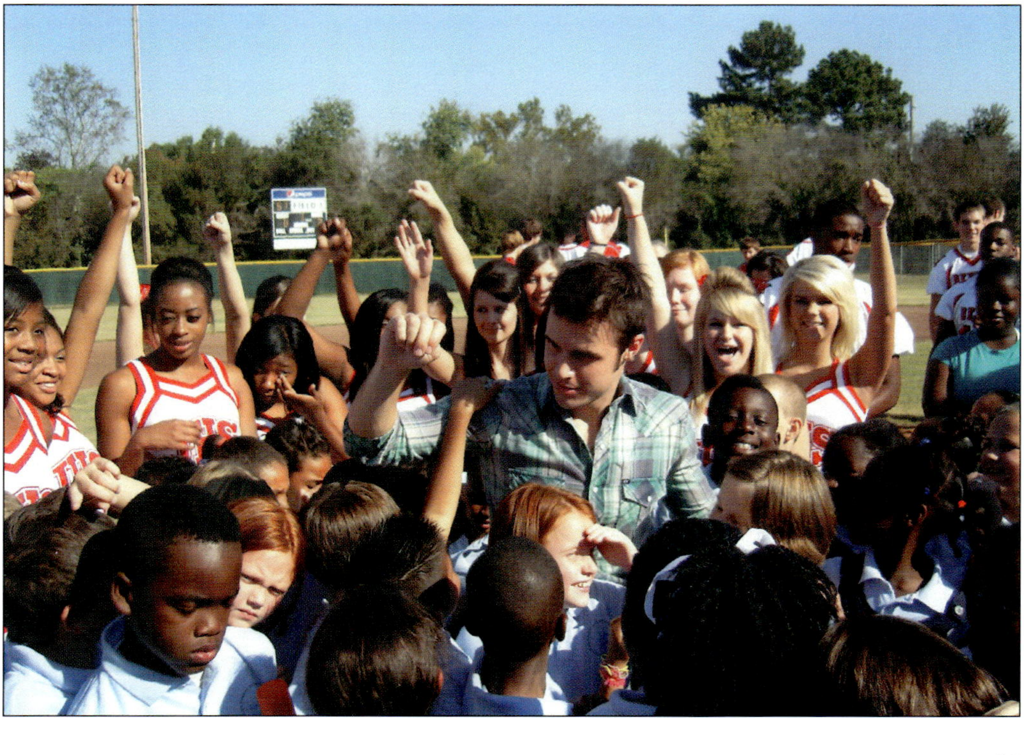

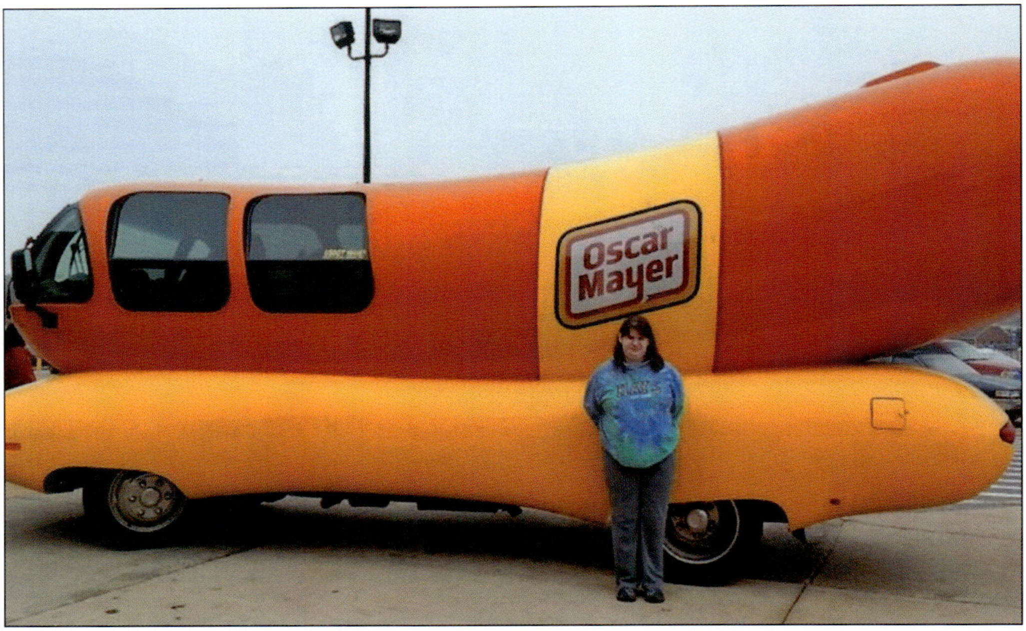

The Wiener Mobile, promoting Oscar Mayer, showed up at the Little Rock Air Force base commissary, and it also made an appearance at the Wal-Mart Super Center in Jacksonville. Everyone was very excited and wanted photographs with unique vehicle. The lady pictured here is Christina Matthews, posing in the Wal-Mart parking lot. (Courtesy of the Jacksonville Historical District.)

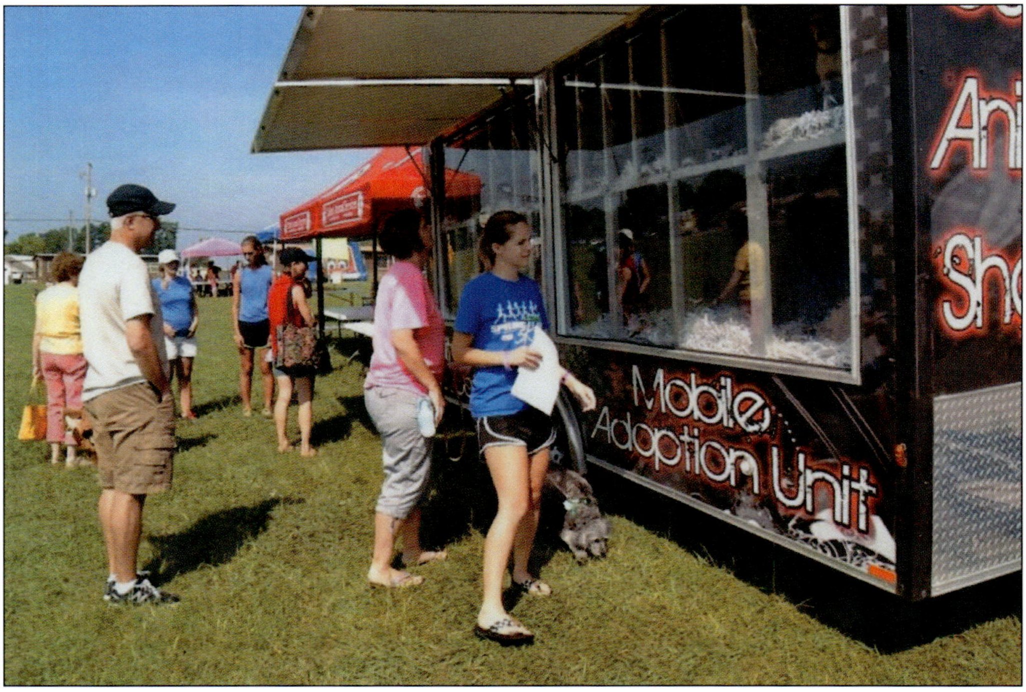

FestiVille patrons look at pets available for adoption from the animal shelter's mobile adoption unit. People take in the sights at Dupree Park with fun and games, rides, and food. There is something for everyone at the two-day the FestiVille. (Courtesy of the City of Jacksonville.)

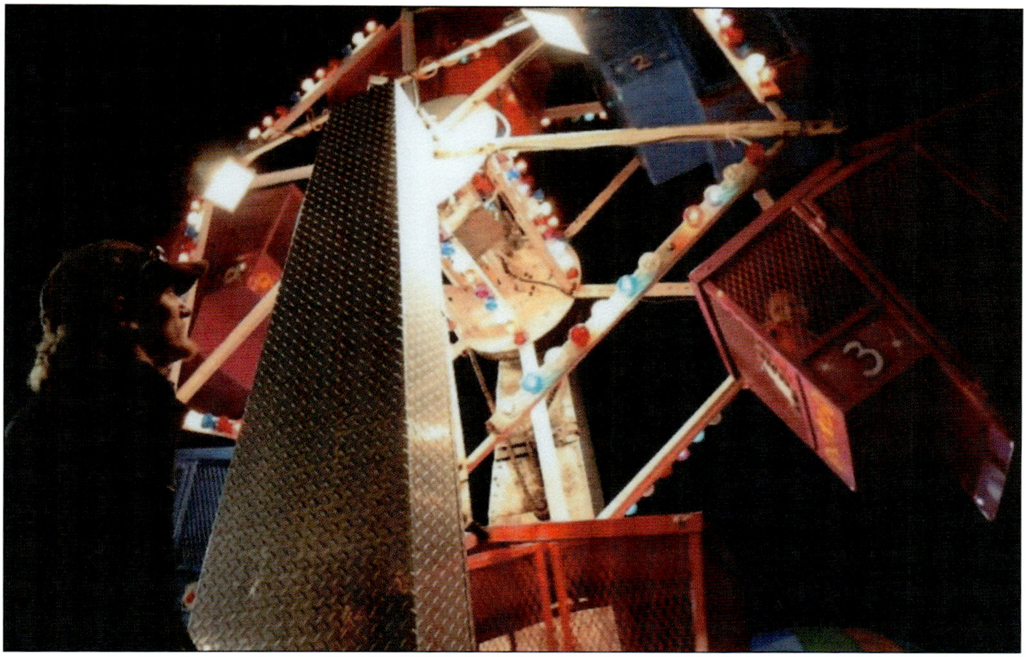

Kevin Carter with Fun Time Shows from Doniphan, Missouri, operates the miniature Ferris wheel, while Lily Hampton enjoys the ride at the Knight's Super Foods parking lot in Jacksonville. (Courtesy of David Scolli.)

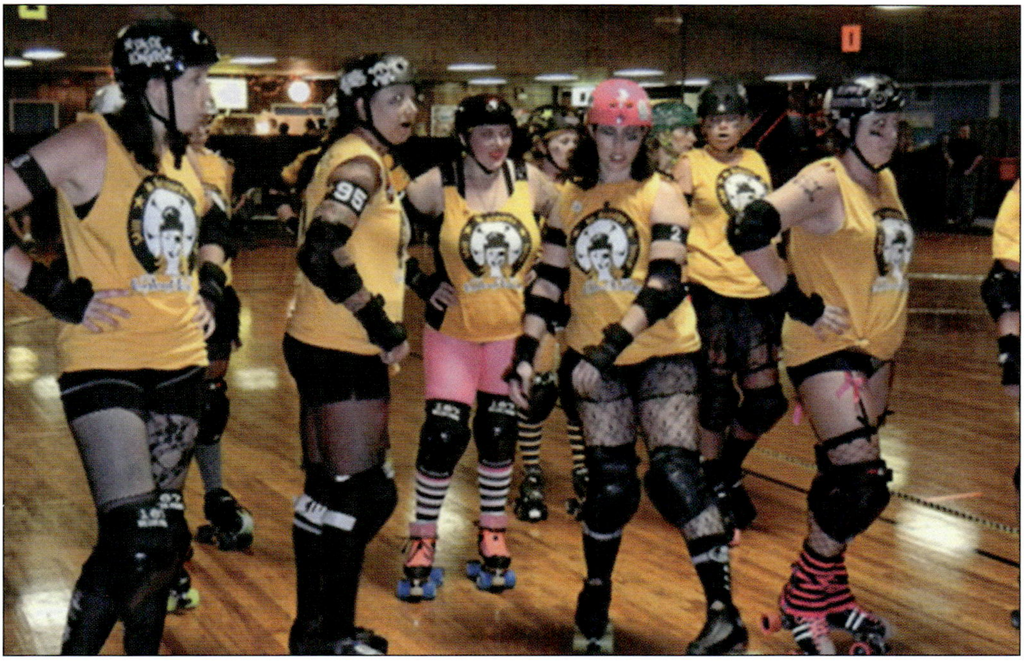

Skateworld of Jacksonville was owned by Raymond F. Ellis. Located at 521 North J.P. Wright Loop Road, at one time it was the place to hang out with friends, with all-night skating or birthday parties. It closed its doors in 2012 with a second owner. This roller-derby team practices at the skating rink. (Courtesy of the Jacksonville Historical District.)